AYATULLAH MURTAZA MUTAHHARI

Ashura – Misrepresentations and Distortions

Copyright © 2021 by Ayatullah Murtaza Mutahhari

All rights reserved. No part of this publication may be reproduced, stored or transmitted in any form or by any means, electronic, mechanical, photocopying, recording, scanning, or otherwise without written permission from the publisher. It is illegal to copy this book, post it to a website, or distribute it by any other means without permission.

First edition

ISBN: 978-1-956276-02-2

This book was professionally typeset by al-Burāq.
Find out more at al-Buraq.org

Contents

1 First Sermon: 'Ashura - History and Popular Legend	1
2 Second Sermon: 'Ashura - History and Popular Legend	26
The Factors of Tahrif	27
The Second Factor	28
The Third Factor	32
3 Third Sermon 'Ashura - Misrepresentations and Distortions	49
Distortions of Meaning	50
How is the Meaning of Events and Facts Distorted?	52
The Character of A Sacred Movement	53
4 Fourth Sermon: 'Ashura - Popular Distortions and our...	69
Our Responsibility and Mission:	78
The Duty of the 'Ulama and the People:	79

One

First Sermon: Ashura – History and Popular Legend

In the Name of Allah, the Beneficent, the Merciful

All Praise belongs to Allah, the Lord of the worlds and the Maker of all creation, and may Peace and benedictions be upon His servant and messenger, His beloved and elect, our master, our prophet, and our sire, Abul Qasim Muhammad, may Allah bless him and his pure, immaculate, and infallible Progeny.

I seek the refuge of Allah from the accursed Satan

> *"So for their breaking their compact We cursed them and made their hearts hard; they would pervert the words from their meanings. And they forgot a portion of what they were reminded of." (5:13)*

Our discussion here concerns the misrepresentations (*tahrifat*) relating to the historic event of *Karbala'*. There have occurred various kinds of distortions in recounting the details of this great event. We shall carry out this discussion in four parts.

The first will deal with the meaning of *tahrif* and its various existing forms, while pointing out that such misrepresentations have occurred in the [popular] accounts of the historic episode of '*Ashura*'.

The second part deals with the general factors responsible for *tahrif*, that is, the causes which commonly lead to the distortion of events and issues in the world. Why do men misrepresent and distort events, issues, and, occasionally, personalities?

In particular, what factors have played a distorting role in the narrative of the episode of *Karbala*'? The third part consists of an explanation concerning the distortions that have crept into the narratives of this historic event. The fourth part deals with ours and our scholars' duty and the Muslim masses, in this regard.

The first part of this discussion is about the meaning of *tahrif*: What does *tahrif* mean? The Arabic word *tahrif* is derived from *harrafa* meaning, to slant, incline, alter, distort, misconstrue which means to make something depart from its original or proper course and position. In other words, *tahrif* is a kind of change and alteration, though it includes a sense not possessed by mere change and alteration.

If you do something that prevents a sentence, message, verse, or passage from conveying the meaning that it ought to convey and gives it some other sense, you have subjected it to *tahrif*. For instance, you make a statement before someone. Elsewhere he quotes you, and later on you are told that so-and-so has reported that you have made such a statement.

You find out that what you had said was very different from what he has reported. He has interpolated your statement, deleting words which conveyed your intent and adding others on his own account, with the result that your statements have been distorted and totally altered. Then you would say that this person has misrepresented your statements especially, if someone tampers with an official document, he is said to be guilty of causing *tahrif* in it.

These examples were meant to elucidate the meaning of the term *tahrif*, and it does not need any further explanation or clarification. Now we shall take up the different forms of *tahrif*.

There are various kinds of *tahrif*, the most important of which are *tahrif* in words and *tahrif* of meaning. *Tahrif* of wording occurs when the literal form of a statement is changed. For instance, when words and phrases are deleted or added to a statement or the sequence of sentences is altered in such a manner as to change its meaning. In this case *tahrif* occurs in the outward form and wording of a statement *Tahrif* of meaning occurs when one does not change the words, which remain in their original form, but the statement is interpreted in a manner that is contrary to the intent of its speaker. It is interpreted in such a manner as to express one's own intent, not that of its author.

The Noble Qur'an employs the term *tahrif* specifically in relation to the Jews. A study of history shows that they have been the champions of *tahrif* throughout the course of history. I don't know what kind of race this is that has such an amazing penchant for misrepresenting facts! Accordingly they always take up professions in which they can distort and misrepresent events.

From what I have heard, the world's well-known news agencies, which are perpetually quoted by the radios and newspapers, are exclusively in the hands of the Jews. Why? Because they can report the events as they wish. How amazing is the Qur'an's statement about them! This characteristic of the Jews, the tendency for *tahrif*, is considered a racial trait by the Qur'an. In one of the verses of the Sura al-Baqarah, the Qur'an declares:

> *"Are you then eager that they (i.e. the Jews) should believe in you, while a party of them had heard Allah's word, and then consciously misinterpreted it, after they had understood it,*

and did that knowingly?" (2:75) [1]

This means, 'O Muslims, have you pinned your hopes on their telling you the truth? They are the same people who would go along with Moses, and hear God's pronouncements. But by the time they returned to their people's midst to recount what they had heard, they would twist it out of shape.' The *tahrif* that they would carry out was not for the reason that they did not understand and so altered what they reported.

No! They are an intelligent people and they understand matters the issues very well. But despite the fact that they understand what they have heard they would recount them in a distorted manner for the people. This is what *tahrif* is, that is, distorting and twisting things out of their original shape-and they carried out *tahrif* even in Divine scriptures!

In this context, in most of the cases the Qur'an uses the very term *tahrif* or expresses the matter in some other manner. However, the exegetes have pointed out that the Qur'anic reference to *tahrif* in this context includes *tahrif* in wording as well as in meaning.

That is, some of the instances of corruption that have occurred [in the scriptures at the hands of the Jews] relating to the wording and some of them relate to the meanings and interpretation. As this involves a digression from my main topic, I do not wish to discuss this matter any further.

There is a story which would not out of place here. One of the scholars

---

[1] J. M Rodwell in his translation of the Qur'an (London: Everyman's Library, p 345) makes in a footnote the following remark under this verse: "This is one of the passages which shows great familiarity with the habit of the Jews on the part of Muhammad." [Tr.]

used to recount that once during the day of his youth a *maddah*[2] from Tehran was visiting Mashhad. During the day he would stand in the Gawharshad Mosque or in the courtyard of the shrine and recite verses and eulogies. Among things that he recited was the famous ghazal ascribed to Hafiz:

O heart!
Be slave of the world's King and rejoice!
Forever dwell in the shelter of God's grace!
Embrace the tomb of Rida, the Eighth Imam,
From the heart's depth, and cling to the threshold of his shrine (*bargah*).

This gentleman, in order to have some fun with him, had approached him and said to him, "Why do you recite this verse wrongly? It should be read like this, which means; as soon as you reach the shrine you must throw yourself down in the manner a bundle of straw (*barekah*) is rolled off the back of an ass."

Thereafter, whenever the poor *maddah* recited these verses, he would say bar-e kah instead of bargah and at the same time throw himself down on the ground! This is what *tahrif* does!

Here I must point out that *tahrif* also differs in respect of the subject involved. There is a time when *tahrif* occurs in an ordinary speech, as when two persons misrepresent each other's words. But there are times when *tahrif* takes place in a matter of great significance to society, such as when there is misrepresentation of eminent personalities.

There are personalities whose words and deeds represent a sacred authority for the people and whose character and conduct is a model for mankind. For instance, if someone were to ascribe to Imam 'Ali (a)

---

[2] The professional maddah, himself somewhat of a rawdeh khwan, though mostly without a clerics training, is someone who recites elegies, verses and even delivers a rawdah in the majalis, the gatherings that are held for the sake of ceremonial mourning, before the rawdeh e khawn takes to the minbar.[Tr.]

a statement that he did not make or something that he had not meant to say, that is very dangerous.

The same is true if a characteristic or trait is ascribed to the Prophet (S) or one of the Imams ('a) when in fact they had some other qualities, or when *tahrif* occurs in a great historic event which serves as a moral and religious authority and as a momentous document from the viewpoint of society's norms and is a criterion in matters of morality and education. It is a matter of incalculable importance and entails a crucial danger when *tahrif*-whether in respect of words or meaning-occurs in subjects which are not of the ordinary kind.

There is a time when someone tampers with a verse of Hafiz or makes interpolations in an animal fable. This is not so important, though, of course one should not tamper with books of literary value.

One professor wrote a paper about *Mush-o gorbeh* ("The Cat and the Mouse"), which is a book of considerable literary value. He had found that it had been victim of so many interpolations, changes of wording, addition and deletion of verses, as to be beyond reckoning. There, he remarks that in his opinion no nation in the whole world is so untrustworthy as the Iranians who have made such extensive unauthorized interpolations in works belonging to their literary heritage.

The same is true of *Rumi's Mathnavi*. God knows how many verses have been appended to the *Mathnawi*! For instance, there is a fine couplet in the original versions of the *Mathnawi* about the power of love. It says:

Love sweetens matters bitter, Love turns bronzes into gold.

That is a sensible thing to say: love is something that turns even the bitter aspects of life into ones that are sweet and pleasant. Love, like an elixir, transforms the bronze of man's being into gold. Then others came and added verses to this one, without bothering for pertinence or aptness in respect of analogy.

For instance, they said: 'Love turns a serpent into an ant,' or that 'love turns the roof into a wall,' or 'love turns a musk-melon into a water-melon'!

These analogies have no relation at all to the theme. Of course such a thing should not happen, but these interpolations do not harm a society's life and felicity and do not cause deviance in its course. But when *tahrif* occurs in things that relate to the people's morality and religion, it is dangerous, and this danger is incalculable when it occurs in documents and matters that constitute the foundations of human life.

The event of *Karbala'* is, inevitably, an event possessing great social meaning for us, and it has a direct impact on our morality and character.

It is an event that prompts our people, without anyone compelling them, to devote millions of man-hours to listening to the related episodes and to spend millions of dollars for this purpose. This event must be retold exactly as it occurred and without the least amount of interpolation. For if the smallest amount of interpolation takes place at our hands in this event, that would distort it, and instead of benefiting from it we would definitely suffer harm.

Now my point is that we have introduced thousands of distortions in retelling the narrative of *Ashura*, both in its outward form, that is, in respect of the very episodes and issues relating to the major events and the minor details, as well as in respect of their interpretation and meaning. Most regrettably, this event has been distorted both in its form and content.

At times a distorted version has at least some resemblance to the original. But there are times when distortion is so thorough that the corrupted version has not the least resemblance to the original: the matter is not only distorted, but it is inverted and turned into its antithesis.

Again I must say with utmost regret that the misrepresentations that have been carried out by us have all been in the direction of degrading and distorting the event and making it ineffective and inert in our lives. In this regard both the orators and scholars of the *ummah* as well as the people have been guilty, and, God willing, we will elucidate all these matters.

Here I will cite examples of some of the distortions that have occurred in the outer form of this event and the concoctions that have grown around it. The topic is so vast as to be beyond expression. It is so vast that should we attempt to collect all the unfounded narratives it will perhaps take several volumes of 500 pages each.

Marhum Hajji Mirza Husayn Nuri, may God elevate his station, was the teacher of such figures as marhum Hajj Shaykh 'Abbas Qummi, *marhum* Haji Shaykh 'Ali Akbar Nehawandi and *marhum* Hajj Shaykh Muhammad Baqir Birjandi. He was a very extraordinary man and a *muhaddith* (scholar of *hadith*) with an unparalleled command of his field and a prodigious memory. He was a man of fine spirituality with a highly fervent and passionate faith.

Although some of the books that he wrote were not worthy of his station[3] -and for this reason he earned the reproach of his contemporary scholars -but in general his books are good, especially the one that he wrote on the topic of the *minbar* (pulpit), entitled *Lu'lu' wa marjan*. Though a small book, it is an excellent work in which he speaks about the duties of those who deliver sermons and recount for the mourners the narrative of *Karbala'* from the minbar. The entire book consists of two parts.

One part is about the sincerity of intention and purpose, as one of the

---

[3] This is a reference to his controversial book Fasl al-Khitab in which he, contrary to the general belief of Shi'i Imami scholars through the course of history, raised doubts concerning the occurrence of tahrif (mainly the occurrence of deletions) in the Qur'an.[Tr.]

requirement for a speaker, orator, sermonizer, and *rawdeh-khwan*[4] is that the motive of someone who relates the narrative of *'Ashura'* should not be greed or attainment of pecuniary gain. How well he has discussed this topic!

The second requirement is honesty and truthfulness. Here, he elaborates on the topic of false and true narration, discussing various forms of lying in such a thorough-going manner that I do not think there is any other book which deals with lying and its various form in the way that it does, and perhaps there is no such other book in the whole world. In it he exhibits a marvelous learning and scholarship.

In this book, that great man mentions several examples of falsehoods that have become prevalent in narratives of the historic event of *Karbala'*. Those which I will mention are all or mostly the same things that the marhum haji Nuri has lamented about.

This great man even says explicitly, "Today too we must mourn Husayn, but there are tragedies which have befallen Husayn in our era which did not occur in the past, and they are all these falsehoods that are said regarding the event of *Karbala'* and which no one opposes! One must shed tears for the sufferings of Husayn ibn 'Ali, not for the sake of the swords and spears that struck his noble body on that day, but on account of these falsehoods." In the book's introduction he writes that an eminent scholar from India had written him a letter complaining about the false narratives that are recited in India, and asking him to do something or to write a book to stop the fictitious narratives that were current there.

Then he remarks: "This Indian scholar has imagined that the *rawdakhwans* tell false stories when they go to India. He does not know

---

[4] The rawdeh-khawn, often a cleric is someone who delivers the rawdah, consisting of narratives relating in particular to the martyrdom of Imam Husayn, his family and companions, and in general to the ordeals of Ahlal Bayt, the Prophet's family. Wa'iz, Dhakir, Minbari, etc. are other names for the professional rawdeh-khwan.

that the stream is polluted from its very source. The centre of false *rawdahs* are *Karbala'*, *Najaf* and *Iran*, that is, the very centre of Shi'ism."

Now as a sample, I will cite some instances of *tahrif*, of which a few relate to the events that occurred before *'Ashura'*, some that occurred during the Imam's way, some during the days of his final halt at *Karbala'* in the month of Muharram.

I will also mention some of them that relate to the days of his family's captivity and some about the Imams who lived after the event of *Karbala'*. However, most of them will relate to the day of *'Ashura'* itself. Now I will give two examples of each of them.

It is essential to mention a point at first, and that is that the people are responsible in all these cases. You folks who attend the majalis[5] sessions imagine that you have no responsibility in this regard, and think that it is only the speakers who are responsible. The people have two major responsibilities.

The first is that of *nahy 'anil-munkar* (forbidding what is wrong) which is obligatory for all. When they find out and know-and most of the time they do know!-that a narrative is untrue, they should not sit in that gathering. It is forbidden to sit in such gatherings and one must protest against them.

Secondly, they must try to get rid of the eagerness and expectation which the hosts as well as the audience attending the majalis have for the majlis to become fervid, that there should be impassioned mourning and the majlis should get feverish with cries of the mourners. The poor speaker knows that if he were to say only things that are true and authentic, the majlis would not get into a frenzy and the same people will not invite him again. Hence he is compelled to add something.

---

[5] The verse pertains to the story of Moses at the time of his flight from Egypt: So he departed therefrom, fearful and vigilant; he said, 'My Lord, deliver me from the wrongdoers.' And when he turned his face towards Midian, he said, 'It may be that my Lord will guide me on the right way.' Quran, 28:21-22

First Sermon: Ashura – History and Popular Legend

The people should get this expectation out of their heads and refrain from encouraging the kind of fictitious narratives which kill the soul of *Karbala* but work up the mourners into a frenzy. The people should hear the true narrative so that their understanding and level of thinking is elevated.

They should know that if a sentence creates a tremor in one's souls and attunes it with the spirit of Husayn ibn 'Ali and, as a result, one small tear were to come out of one's eyes, it is really a precious station. But tears drawn by the scenes of mere butchery, even if a deluge, are worthless.

They say that in one of the towns there was an eminent scholar who had some concern for the faith and who protested against these falsehoods which are uttered from the minbar. He would say, "What are these abominable things that they say on the minbar?" One wa'iz said to him, "If we don't say these things we will have to shut down our shops right away!" That gentleman replied, "These are mendacities and one must not utter them."

By chance, some days later this gentleman himself happened to host a majlis in his mosque and he invited the same waiz; to make the rawdah. But before his taking his seat on the minbar the host said to the wa'iz, "I want to hold a model majlis in which nothing is said except the true narrative. Make it a point not to recount any episode except out of the reliable books.

You shouldn't touch any of that abominable stuff!' The wai'z replied, "The majlis is hosted by you. Your will, will be done." On the first night, the gentleman himself sat there facing the qiblah in the prayer niche, close to the minbar. The wai'z; began his sermon, and when the time came to recite the tragic narrative, as he had committed himself to recite nothing but the true accounts, the majlis remained unmoved and frozen as he spoke on.

The gentleman was now upset. He was the host of the majlis and he thought about what the people would say behind his back. The women would certainly say, "To be sure, the Aqa's intent was not sincere, and so the majlis was a fiasco."

Had his intentions been good and were his motives sincere the majlis would have been rocked with the howls and-groans of mourners crying their eyes out. He saw that it would all end up in a loss of face. What should he do? Quietly, he signaled to the wai'z, "Get a bit of that abominable stuff!"

The expectation of the people that the majlis should go wild with mourning is itself a source of falsehoods. Accordingly, most of the fabrications that have occurred have been for the purpose of drawing tears, nothing else.

I have heard this story repeatedly, and you too must have heard it. Hajji Nuri also mentions it. They say that one day 'Ali, the Commander of the Faithful, may Peace be upon him, was delivering a sermon from the *minbar*. Suddenly Imam Husayn ('a) said, 'I am thirsty, Imam 'Ali said, 'Let someone bring water for my son.' The first person to get up was a little boy, Abu al-Fadl al-'Abbas ('a). He went out and got a jar of water from his mother.

When he returned carrying the jar on his head, his head was drenched in water as it spilled from the sides. This story is narrated in its elaborate detail. Then, when the Commander of the Faithful's eyes fell on this scene, tears flowed from his eyes. He was asked why he was crying. He told them that the ordeals that this young son of his would face had come to his mind.

You know the rest of the story, which serves the purpose of a point of departure for switching to the tragic scenes of *Karbala'*. Hajji Nuri has an excellent discussion at this point. He writes, "Now that you say that 'Ali was delivering a sermon from the *minbar*, you should know that 'Ali spoke from the *minbar* and delivered sermons only during the period of his caliphate.

Hence, the episode must have occurred in Kufah. At that time Imam Husayn was a man of about thirty-three years." Then he remarks, "Is it at all a sensible thing for a man of thirty-three years to say all of a sudden, in a formal gathering while his father is delivering a sermon, 'I am thirsty!' 'I want water!"

If an ordinary man does such a thing, it would be considered ill-mannered of him. Moreover, Hadrat Abu al-Fadl, too, was not a child at that time but a young man of at least fifteen years." You see how they have fabricated the story! Is such a story worthy of Imam Husayn? Aside from its fictitious character, what value does it have?

Does it elevate the station of Imam Husayn or does it detract from it? It is definitely detracting to the dignity of the Imam, as it ascribes a false act to the Imam and detracts from is station by bringing the Imam down to the level of a most ill-mannered person who, at a time when his father -a man like 'Ali -is delivering a sermon, feels thirsty and instead of waiting for the session to be over, suddenly interrupts his father's sermon to ask for water.'

Another example of such fabrications is the story of a messenger who has brought a letter for Abu 'Abd Allah ('a) and he awaits a reply. The Imam tells him to come after three days and collect the reply. After three days on inquiring he is told that the Imam was departing the same day.

He says to himself, "Now that he is setting out, let us go and watch the majesty and glamour of the prince of the Hijaz He goes and there he sees the Imam, together with other Hashimis among men, seated on splendid chairs. Then the camels are brought bearing the litters draped in silk and brocade.

Then the ladies emerge and with much honor and ceremony they are escorted into these litters. This description continues in this vein until they make the digression to switch to the scene of the eleventh day of Muharram, to compare the glamour and honor of this day with the sorry state of the womenfolk on the latter day. Haji Nuri calls such descriptions into question. He says, "It is history which says that when Imam Husayn left Madinah he recited this Qur'anic verse:

"He left it in the state of fear and concern". (28:21)

That is, he likened his own departure to that of Moses, son of 'Imran, when he fled for the fear of the Pharaoh.

"He said, "It might be that my Lord will guide me to the right path.""(28:22)

The Imam had departed with a most simple caravan. Does the greatness of Imam Husayn lie in his sitting, for instance, on golden chairs? Or does the greatness of his family and womenfolk lie in their using litters draped in silk and brocade, or their possessing fine horses and camels and a retinue of lackeys and servants?!

Another example of *tahrif* in the accounts of *'Ashura'* is the famous story of Layla, the mother of Hadrat 'Ali' Akbar, a story that is not supported even by a single work of history. Of course, Ali' Akbar had a mother whose name was Layla, but not a single historical work has stated that Layla was present at *Karbala'*. But you see how many pathetic tales there are about Layla and Ali' Akbar, including the story of Layla's arrival at 'Ali Akbar's side at the time of his martyrdom.

I have heard this story even in Qum, in a majlis that had been held on behalf of Ayatullah Burujerdi, though he himself was not attending. In this tale, as 'Ali Akbar leaves for the battlefield the Imam says to Layla, "I have heard from my grandfather that God answers a mother's prayer for the sake of her child. Go into a solitary tent, unfurl your locks and pray for your son. It may be that God will bring our son safe back to us."

First of all, there was no Layla in *Karbala'* to have done that. Secondly, this was not Husayn's logic and way of thinking. Husayn's logic on the day of 'Ashara' was the logic of self-sacrifice. All historians have written that whenever anyone asked the Imam for the leave to go to battlefield, the Imam would at first try to restrain him with some excuse or another that he could think of, excepting the case of 'Ali' Akbar about whom they write:

Thereat he asked his father's permission to go forth to fight, and he gave him the permission.[6]

That is, as soon as 'Ali Akbar asked for permission, the Imam told him to depart. Nevertheless, there is no dearth of verses which depict the episode in quite a different light, including this one:

Rise, O father, let us leave this wilderness, Let us go now to Layla's tent.

Another case relating to the same story, which is also very amazing, is the one that I heard in Tehran. It was in the house of one of the eminent scholars of this city where one of the speakers narrated the story of Layla. It was something which I had never heard in my life.

According to his narrative, after Layla went into the tent, she opened the locks of her hair and vowed that if God were to bring 'Ali Akbar back safely to her and should he not be killed in *Karbala'* she would sow basil (*rayhan*) all along the way from *Karbala'* to Madinah, a distance of 300 parasangs. Having said this, he began to sing out this couplet:

I have made a vow, were they to return I will sow basil all the way to Taft!

This Arabic couplet caused me greater surprise as to where it came from. On investigating I found that the Taft mentioned in it is not *Karbala'* but a place related to the famous love legend of Layla and Majnun. Taft was the place where the legendary Layla live. This couplet

---

[6] Ibn Tawus, al-Luhuf, p. 47

was composed by Majnun al-'Amiri and sung for the love of Layla, and here this man was reciting it while attributing it to Layla, the mother of 'Ali Akbar, conjuring a fictitious connection with *Karbala'*.

Just imagine, were a Christian or a Jew, or for that matter some person with no religious affiliation, were to be there and hear these things, will he not say what a nonsensical hagiography these people have? He would not know that this tale has been fabricated by that man, but he would say, *na'udubillah*, how senseless were the women saints of this people to vow sowing basil from *Karbala'* to Madinah!

A worse fabrication is the one mentioned by Hajji Nuri. As you know, in the heat of the battle on the day of 'Ashura', the Imam offered his prayers hurriedly in the form of *salat al-khawf*[7] and there was no respite even to offer full prayers. In fact, two of the companions of the Imam came to stand in front of him to shield the Imam (against the arrows) so that he may offer two rak'ahs of the *salat al-khawf*.

The two of them fell from the injuries inflicted under the shower of the arrows. The enemy would not even give respite for offering prayers. Nevertheless, they have concocted a story that the Imam called for a wedding ceremony on this day, declaring, 'It is my wish to see one of my daughter wedded to Qasim.' Obviously, one cannot take one's wishes to one's grave.

By God, see what kind of things they have attributed to a man like Husayn ibn 'Ali, things the like of which we sometimes hear from persons of a very mediocre character, who express a wish to see the wedding of their son or daughter in their life. And this is said to have occurred at a time when there was hardly any respite even for offering prayers.

---

[7] The Shari'ah stipulates certain modifications in the obligatory salat, the daily ritual prayers, when offered in conditions of war and danger of the enemy's attack. The salat thus offered is referred to as salat al-khawf; (see the Quran, 4:101). [Tr.]

They say that the Hadrat said, 'I want to wed my daughter to my nephew here and now, even if it is just an appearance of a wedding.' One of the things that was an inseparable part of our traditional *ta'ziyahs* was the wedding of Qasim, the boy bridegroom.

Such an episode is not mentioned in any reliable book of history. According to Hajji Nuri, Mulla Husayn Kashifi was the first man to write this story in a book named *Rawdat al-shuhada'* and it is totally fictitious. The case here is similar to the one about which the poet says:

Many are the appendages that they have clapped upon it, You will hardly recognize it when you see it again.

Were the Sayyid al-Shuhada' to come and observe these things (and, of course, he does from the world of the spirit, but were he come into the world of appearance) he will find that we have carved out for him companions that he never had.

For instance, in the book *Muhriq al-qulub* -whose author was, incidentally, an eminent scholar and jurist, but who had no knowledge of these matters -that one of the companions to appear out of nowhere on the day of 'Ashura' was Hashim Mirqal, who came bearing an eighteen cubits long spear in his hand.

(After all someone had claimed that Sinan ibn Anas -who according to some reports severed the head of Imam Husayn -had a spear sixty cubits long. He was told that a spear could not be sixty cubits. He replied that God had sent it for him from the heaven!) *Muhriq al-qulub* writes that Hashim ibn 'Utbah Mirqal appeared with a spear sixteen cubits long, whereas this Hashim ibn 'Utbah was a companion of Amir al-Mu'minin 'Ali and had been killed twenty years earlier.

We have attributed several companions to Husayn ibn 'Ali that he did not have, such as the Za'far the Jinn. Similarly, there are some names among the enemies that did not exist. It is mentioned in the book *Asrar al-shahadah* that 'Umar ibn Sa'd's army in *Karbala'* consisted of one million and sixty thousand men. One may ask, where did they come from? Were they all Kufans? Is such a thing possible?

It is also written in that book that Imam Husayn himself personally killed three hundred thousand men in combat. The bomb that destroyed Hiroshima killed sixty thousand people. I calculated that if we assume that a swordsman kills one man every second, it would take eighty-three hours and twenty minutes to massacre a force of three hundred thousand.

Later, when they saw that this number of those felled by the Imam did not fit with a day's duration, they said that the day of *'Ashura* was also seventy-two hours long!

Similar things are said concerning Hadrat Abu al-Fadl, that he killed twenty-five thousand men. I calculated that if one man were killed per second, it would require six days and fifty and odd hours to kill that many.

Therefore, we have to admit what Hajji Nuri, this great man, says, that if one wanted to mourn the Imam today and narrate the ordeals of Abu 'Abd Allah, may Peace be upon him, one should lament over these new tragedies, over these falsehoods, which have been incorporated in the accounts of his martyrdom.

Another example relates to the day of *'Arba'in*. At the time of *'Arba'in* everyone relates the narrative that leads the people to imagine that the captives of the Imam's family arrived at *Karbala'* on the day of *'Arba'in*, and that Imam Zayn al-'Abidin met Jabir (ibn 'Abd Allah al-Ansari) there. However, excepting the *Luhuf*, whose author is Sayyid ibn Tawus and who has denied it in his other books, or at least has not confirmed it, such an episode is not mentioned in any other book, nor does it seem very reasonable to believe it.

But is it possible to expunge these stories, which are repeated every year, from the people's minds? Jabir was the first visitor to Imam Husayn grave, and the significance of *'Arba'in* is also nothing except that it is the occasion for the *ziyarah* of Imam Husayn's tomb.

It is not for the renewal of mourning for the Ahl al-Bayt, nor on account of their arrival in *Karbala'*. Basically, the road to Madinah from Syria is not through *Karbala'* and the two ways diverge from Syria itself.

What is more painful is that, incidentally, there are few events in history that are as rich as the event of *Karbala'* from the viewpoint of reliable sources. Formerly I used to imagine that the basic reason for the proliferation of legends in this field is that the actual events are not known to anybody. But when I studied I found that no event of remote past-for instance of a period thirteen or fourteen centuries ago-has as reliable an history as the event of *Karbala'*.

Reliable Muslim historians have reported the pertinent episodes with trustworthy chains of transmission from the first/seventh and the second/eighth centuries, and their narrations are close and corroborate one another.

There were certain reasons which were responsible for the preservation of these details in history. One of them, which caused the details of this event to be preserved and its objectives to remain clear, were the many speeches (*khutbahs*) that were delivered during its course. In those days, an oration was what communiqués and press releases are in our era.

In the same way that official communiques issued during wartime are the best historical source, so were orations in these days. Accordingly, there were many of them before the event of *Karbala'*, during, and after it. Individuals from among the Prophet's household made orations in Kufah, Damascus and other places.

Basically, their aim by delivering these orations was to inform the people about the episodes as well as to declare the truth of the matter and to spell out the goals. This was itself one of the reason for the events to be reported.

There were also many exchanges, questions and answers, in the event of *Karbala'* and these are recorded in history. They too disclose for us the nature of the occurrences.

Rajaz poetry[8] was also recited a lot during *Karbala'*, and, in particular Abu 'Abd Allah ('a) himself recited much *rajaz*, and these *rajaz* verses also reveal the character of the confrontation.

There were many letters that were exchanged before and after the episode of *Karbala'*, letters that were exchanged between the Imam and the people of Kufah, between the Imam and the people of Basrah, the letters that the Imam wrote earlier to Mu'awiyah (which indicate that the Imam was preparing for an uprising after Mu'awiyah's death), the letters that the enemies wrote to one another, Yazid to Ibn Ziyad, Ibn Ziyad to Yazid, Ibn Ziyad to 'Umar ibn Sa'd, 'Umar ibn Sa'd to Ibn Ziyad, whose texts are all recorded in the history of Islam.

Hence the developments relating to *Karbala'* are quite clear and all of them are throughout a matter of great honor and pride. But we have disfigured this shining historic event to such an extent and have committed such a monstrous treachery towards Imam Husayn ('a) that if he were to come and see, he will say, 'You have changed the entire face of the event.

I am not the Imam Husayn that you have sketched out in your own imagination. The Qasim ibn Hasan that you have painted in your fancy is not my nephew. The 'Ali Akbar that you have faked in your imagination is not my aware and intelligent son. The companions that you have carved out are not my companions."

We have fabricated a Qasim whose only desire is to become a bridegroom and whose uncle's wish, too, is to have him wedded. Contrast this one with the historical Qasim. Reliable histories report that on the night of *'Ashura'* the Imam ('a) gathered his companions in a

---

[8] It was a tradition among the Arab warriors to recite verses during combat and encounter with the enemy on the battlefield. Rajaz is the form of poetry composed of such purposes and occasions. [Tr.]

tent whose location, as described by the phrase '*inda qurbil-ma*',⁹ was the place where water used to be kept, or near it.

There he delivered that very well-known sermon of the night preceding '*Ashura*'. I do not want to mention its details here, but, to put it briefly, in this sermon the Imam told them that every one of them was free to depart and leave him to confront the enemy alone.

The Imam did not want anybody to stay just for considerations of courtesy or to remain out of compulsion, or even to think that they were obliged to do so by virtue of the allegiance (*bay'ah*) they had given him.

Hence he tells them, "You are all free, my companions, members of my family, my sons, and my nephews-everyone-to leave without being liable to anything. They [i.e. the enemy's forces] have nothing against anyone except me. The night is dark.

Take advantage of the darkness of the night and depart. They will definitely not stop you." At first, he expresses his appreciation for them and tells them, I am most pleased with you. I do not know of any companions better than mine, and no better relatives than the members of my family."

But all of them tell him, in unison, that such a thing was impossible. What answer will they give to the Prophet on the Day of Resurrection? What will happen to loyalty, to humanity, to love and attachment? Their ardent responses and their words said on that occasion melt a heart of stone and are most moving.

One of them says, "Is one life worth enough to be sacrificed for someone like you? I wish that I were brought to life seventy times to die seventy times for your sake." Another says, "I would lay down

---

⁹ Bihar al-Anwar, vol. 44 p. 392, A'lam al-Wara, p. 234, al-Shaykh al-Mufid, Kitab al-Irshad, p. 231, al-Muqarrim, Maqtal al-Husayn, p. 257. Apparently, there was a tent where water-skins used to be kept and stored from the first days of the caravan's halt at Karbala'.

a thousand lives for your sake if I had them." Another says, "If I were to sacrifice my life for you and my body were burnt to ashes and the ashes were cast to wind, and were this done a hundred times, I would still love to die for your sake."

The first to speak was his brother Abu al-Fadl, and then the Imam changed the subject and told them about the events of the next day, informing them that they all would be killed. All of them receive it as great good news.

Now this young man -to whom we are so unjust and think that all that he cherished in his heart was the wish to become a bridegroom -puts a question to the Imam. In reality he expresses his real wish. When a group of elderly men gather in an assembly, a boy of thirteen does not sit in their midst, but reverently stays behind them.

It appears that this youth was sitting behind the Imam's elderly companions and was keen to hear what others said. When the Imam told them that they would all be killed on the next day, this child wondered if he too would be one of them. He thought to himself, after all I am only a boy. Perhaps the Imam means that only the elderly would be martyred. I am just a minor." Therefore, he turned to the Imam and asked him:

Will I be among those who will be killed?

Look! See what his wish and aspiration are! The Imam says to him, "Qasim, first let me ask you a question. I will reply after you have answered me." I think the Imam purposefully put this question. With this question he wanted to show to posterity that they shouldn't think that this youth gave his life without awareness and understanding, that they should not imagine that what he cherished was a wish to become bridegroom, that they should not conjure up a wedding for him and be guilty of the crime of distorting his fine character. So the Imam said, "First, I will ask you a question":

That is, "My child, my nephew, tell me, how do you regard death and what do you think about getting killed?' He promptly answered.

"It is sweater to me than honey!"

That is, "I haven't a desire that should be dearer and sweater to me!" This is an astounding scene. These are the things that have made this a great and historic event -and we should keep it alive! For there will not be another Husayn, nor another Qasim ibn Hasan.

These are the things that make us give so much value to this event, and if after fourteen centuries we build such a *husayniyyah* as this[10] in their memory and in their name, we have done nothing. Or else the wish to become bridegroom does not oblige one to put in one's time and money, to build *husayniyyahs* or to deliver sermons. But they were the very essence of humanity, the very concrete instances of the Divine purpose as stated in the verse:

"Surely I will make a vicegerent in the earth" (2:30)

And they stood above the angels.

After getting this answer, the Imam said to him, "My nephew, you too will be killed. But your death will be different from that of others

And (it will be) after you have faced a great ordeal.

Accordingly, when Qasim, after much insistence, received the permission to leave for the battlefield, being very young, there was no armour that was fit for his years, nor a helmet nor shoes, nor arms. It is written that he wore a turban (*'ammamah*) and this description is given of his appearance:

---

[10] This is a reference to the Husayniyyeh-ye Irshad, in Tehran. Husayniyyah is a building which is at times also used as a mosque but is built mainly with the purpose of holding mourning ceremonies during the months of Muharram and Safar as well as other occasions relating to anniversaries of the martyrdom of the figures of the Ahl al-Bayt.

He appeared like a piece of the moon.[11]

This boy was so handsome that when the enemies saw him they described him as a piece of the moon: 'Where does the wind carry this petal of red rose?' said whoever that saw you on your fleeting mount.

The narrator says: "I saw that the strap of one of his sandals was untied, and I do not forget that it was his left foot" This shows that he was not wearing boots. They write that the Imam stood near the tents as he held his horse's reins. Evidently he was alert and ready. At once he heard a cry. It was Qasim: *"Ya 'ammah!"* (O Uncle!).

They write that the Imam flew on the horse like a hunting falcon. As he arrived by the side of this youth, about two hundred men had surrounded this child. They fled as the Imam attacked, and one of the enemy's men who had dismounted to sever Qasim's head was himself trampled under the hoofs of the horses of his fleeing comrades.

The one who is said to have been trampled to death under the hoofs of the horses was one of the enemy's men, not Hadrat Qasim. In any case, when the Imam arrived at Qasims side, there was so much dust and confusion that nobody could see what was happening; when the dust settled down, they saw the Imam sitting at Qasim's side with his head in his arms. They heard the Imam utter this sentence:

My nephew! By God, it is very hard on your uncle that you should call him and he should not be able to respond, or that he should respond without being able to do anything for you![12]

It was at this moment that a cry came from this youth and his spirit departed towards its Creator.

---

[11] Ibn Shahr Ashub, al-Manaqib, iii, p. 106, see also A'lam al-Wara, p.242; al-Luhuf, 48; Bihar al-Anwar, vol 45 p. 35, al-Mufid's Kitab al Irshad, p. 239, al-Muqarrim's Maqtal al-Husayn, p. 331; and al-Tabari's Ta'rikh, vi, p. 256.

[12] Ibn Shahr Ashub, al-Manaqib, iv, p. 107, A'lam al-Wara, p. 243; al-Luhuf, 38; Bihar al-Anwar, vol. 45 p. 35, al-Mufid's Kitab al Irshad, p. 239, al-Muqarrim's Maqtal al-Husayn, p. 332; and al-Tabari's Ta'rikh, vi, p. 257.

O God, may our ultimate end be one that is of felicity. Make us aware of the realities of Islam! Remove from us our ignorance and nescience with Your grace and munificence. Give all of us the ability to act with sincere intentions. Fulfill our legitimate needs and forgive all our dead and pardon them.

Two

Second Sermon: 'Ashura – History and Popular Legend

In the Name of Allah, the Beneficent, the Merciful

All Praise belongs to Allah, the Lord of the worlds and the Maker of all creation, and may Peace and benedictions be upon His servant and messenger, His beloved and elect, our master, our prophet, and our sire, Abu al-Qasim Muhammad, may Allah bless him and his pure, immaculate, and infallible Progeny.

I seek the refuge of Allah from the accursed Satan:

"So for their breaking their compact We cursed them and made their hearts hard; they would pervert the words from their meanings, and they forgot a portion of what they were reminded of." (5:13)

We said that the event of 'Ashura' has been subject to *tahrif* and it has occurred both in its outward form as well as its inner content. A consequence of these distortions has been that this great historic document and this great educative source has become ineffectual or less potent, in our lives, leaving, at times, even an opposite effect.

All of us have the duty to purge it of the distortions that have polluted this sacred document. Tonight we will discuss the general factors responsible for *tahrif*. Thereafter our discussion will focus on *tahrif* in the content and significance of this event.

The Factors of Tahrif

These factors are of two kinds, one of which is of a general nature. That is, there are in general certain factors that lead to the corruption of histories and these are not limited to the event of 'Ashura' alone. For instance, the enemy's motives are themselves a factor that distort an event. In order to achieve their purposes, the enemies bring about alterations in historical texts or misinterpret them. There are many examples of it which I do not wish to mention here.

All that I would say is that this kind of *tahrif* did play a role in distorting the facts of *Karbala'*, and the enemies did take resort in misrepresenting the uprising of Imam Husayn. As usually happens, the enemies accuse sacred movements of causing conflict and division and of disrupting social harmony and peace. The Umayyad regime also made much effort to give such a hue to the Husayni uprising.

Such propaganda began from the very first day. When Muslim arrived in Kufah, Yazid, while sending an order appointing Ibn Ziyad to the governership of Kufah, wrote: "Muslim, son of 'Aqil, has gone to Kufah and his aim is to disrupt peace and to create social discord and disunity in the Muslim community. Go and suppress him."

When Muslim was captured and brought to the *dar al-imarah*, the governor's residency, Ibn Ziyad said to Muslim: "Son of 'Aqil! What was it that brought you to this city? The people here lived in satisfaction and peace.

You came and disrupted their peace, causing disunity and conflict amongst Muslims." Muslim answered in a manly manner and said: "Firstly, I did not come to this city on my own account. It was the people of this city who invited us.

They wrote a great number of letters, which are in our possession. In those letters they wrote that your father, Ziyad, who ruled this city for years, had killed its virtuous men and imposed its scoundrels over the virtuous, subjecting them to various forms of tyranny and injustice. They appealed to us to help them establish justice. We have come to establish justice!"

The Umayyad regime did wage much propaganda of this kind, but their misrepresentations did not affect the history of Islam. You will not find a single competent historian in the world who might have said that Husayn ibn 'Ali, *naudhubillah*, made an unlawful uprising that he rose to cause conflict and disunity among the people. No.

The enemy could not bring about any misrepresentation in [the history of] the event of Karbala'. Most regrettably, whatever *tahrif* has occurred in the event of Karbala' has been at the hands of the friends.

The Second Factor

The second factor is the human tendency towards myth-making and for turning facts into legends. This tendency has been at work in all the world's historical traditions. There is a tendency in men for hero worship which induces the people to fabricate myths and legends about national and religious heroes.[13]

The best evidence of it are the legends that the people have invented around the figures of some geniuses such as Ibn Sina and Shaykh Baha'i. Ibn Sina, undoubtedly, was a genius and was gifted with extraordinary physical and intellectual powers. But these very gifts have led the people

---

[13] During the nights of the 'id of Ghadir, Dr. Shari'ati delivered an excellent lecture on this general human tendency for hero-worship and making of myths and legends, turning historic figures into legendary heroes with extraordinary and superhuman characteristics.

to weave out legends about him.

For instance, it is said that once Ibn Sina saw a man from a distance of one parasang and remarked that the man was eating bread made with oil. They asked him how he could know that the man was eating bread and that it was made with oil.

He replied that he saw flies circling the bread, which had made him conclude that there was oil in the bread. Obviously, this is a legend. Someone who can see flies from the distance of one parasang will see bread made with oil much sooner than he would see flies!

Or it is said that once during the time that Ibn Sina was studying at Isfahan he complained that when he gets up in the middle of the night to study, he was disturbed by the noise of the hammering of the coppersmiths of Kashan.

They went and made a test. One night they told the coppersmiths of Kashan not to use their hammers. That night, said Ibn Sina, he had slept peacefully and was undisturbed in his study. Obviously this is a legend.

Many such legends have been made about Shaykh Bahi'i as well. Such things are not confined to the event of 'Ashura. However, let the people say what they would about Ibn Sina. What harm does it do?

None! But in respect of individuals who are guides of mankind and whose words and deeds and whose stands and uprisings serve as a model and authority, there should not be any *tahrif* whatsoever in their statements, in their personality, and history.

How many legends have been fabricated by us Shi'is about Amir al Mu'minin 'Ali, many Peace be upon him! There is no doubt that 'Ali ('a) was an extraordinary man. No one has doubts about 'Ali's courage which was superior to that of any ordinary human being. 'Ali did not encounter any contestant in battle without felling him to the ground.

But does that satisfy the myth makers? Never! For instance, there is the legend about 'Ali's encounter with Marhab in the battle of Khaybar with all the curious details about the physique of Marhab. The historians have also written that 'Ali's sword cut him into two from the middle (I don't know whether the two halves were perfectly equal!).

But here they found the opportunity to weave out fables which are harmful for the faith. It is said that God commanded Gabriel to go immediately to the earth lest 'Ali's sword when it comes down on Marhab should cut the earth into two halves, reaching right down to the Cow and the Fish.

Gabriel was told to shield the blow with his wings. Gabriel went and when 'Ali struck the blow with his sword, it slashed Marhab into two halves which had they been put in a balance would have turned out to be exactly equal.

However, one of Gabriel's wings suffered injury and he could not ascend to the heaven for forty days. When at last he arrived in heaven, God asked him as to where he had been all these days. He replied, "O Lord! I was on the earth. You had given me an assignment to go there." He was asked why he had taken so much time to return.

Gabriel said, "O God, the blow of 'Ali's sword wounded my wings and I was busy bandaging and healing them all these forty days!" According to another legend 'Ali's sword flew so swiftly and slickly through Marhab's forehead cutting all the way to the saddle that when 'Ali pulled away his sword Marhab himself did not know what had happened (he thought the blow had gone amiss).

He jeered at 'Ali, "Was that all of your swordsmanship?!" 'Ali' said to him, "Just move yourself a bit and see." As soon as Marhab made a movement, one half of his body fell on one side of the horse and the other on the other side!

Hajji Nuri, this great man, in his book *Lu'lu wa marjan*, while condemning the practice of fabricating of such legends, writes about legends that some people have put into circulation concerning the valor of Hadrat Abu al-Fadl al-'Abbas.

According to one of them, in the Battle of *Siffin* (in which, basically, it is not known whether he had participated, and even if he did he must have been a boy of fifteen years) he threw a man into the air, then another, and so on up to eighty men, and by the time the last one was thrown up the first one had not yet reached the ground. Then when the first one came down, he cut him into two halves, then the second and so on to the last man!

A part of the interpolations in the narratives of the event of Karbala have resulted from the myth-making tendency. The Europeans assert that one finds many exaggerations in accounts pertaining to the history of the East, and there is some truth in what they say.

Mulla Darbandi writes in his book *Asrar al-shahadah* that the cavalry of the army of 'Umar ibn Sa'd consisted of six hundred thousand horsemen and twenty million infantrymen -in all a force of one million and six hundred thousand plus all the people of Kufah! Now how large was Kufah?

Kufah was a recently founded city and not more than thirty-five years old, as it was built during the time of 'Umar ibn Khattab. It was built at 'Umar's orders as a military outpost for Muslim warriors near the borders of Iran. It is not certain whether the entire population of Kufah during that time was even a hundred thousand.

That a force of one million and six hundred thousand could have been assembled on that day and that Husayn ibn 'Ali' should have killed three hundred thousand of them is not at all reasonable. Such figures cast a shadow on the whole event.

It is said that someone once made exaggerated claims about the largeness of the city of Herat in former days. He said, 'Herat was a very big city at one time.' 'How big? he was asked. He said, 'At one time there were in Herat twenty thousand one-eyed cooks named Ahmad selling head and totters stew. Now imagine how many men there must be in a city, and how many named Ahmad, and how many one-eyed

Ahmads, to have twenty-one thousand one-eyed Ahmads selling head and totters stew!

This myth-making tendency has always been very active; but we must not leave a sacred document to the mercy of myth-makers.

There is amongst us, the *Ahl al-Bayt*, in every generation reformers who purge the faith of the perversions of the extremists, of the false beliefs of the falsifiers, and of the misinterpretations of the ignorant.[14]

We have a duty here. Now let anyone say anything he likes about Herat. But is it right that such legends as these should find way into the history of the event of *Ashura'*, an event concerning which our duty is to keep it alive and revive its memory every year?

The Third Factor

The third factor is of a particular nature. The two factors that we have discussed above, that is, the hostile ends of the enemies and the human tendency for conjuring legends and myths, apply to all histories of the world, but there is also a factor which is specific to the event of *Ashura'* that has led to fabrication of stories.

The leaders of the faith, from the time of the Noble Messenger and the Pure Imams, have commanded in clear and emphatic terms that the memory of Husayn ibn 'Ali must be kept alive and that his martyrdom and ordeals should be commemorated every year. Why? What is the reason underlying this Islamic ordinance? Why is there so much encouragement for and emphasis on visiting the shrine of Husayn ibn 'Ali?

We should reflect over these questions. Some might say that it is for the sake of condoling with Hadrat Zahra' and offering her consolation! But is it not ridiculous to imagine that Hadrat Zahra' should still

---

[14] Al-Kulayni, Usul al-Kafi, "kitab fadl al-'ilm", p. 32; al-Saffar, Basa'ir al-darajat, p.10

need consolation after fourteen hundred years, whereas, in accordance with the explicit statements of Imam Husayn and according to our creed, since his martyrdom Imam Husayn and Hadrat Zahra have been together in heaven?

What a thing to say! Is it correct to think of Hadrat Zahra as a little child that goes on weeping, even after fourteen centuries, and whom we have to go and console? Such kind of belief is destructive for religion. Imam Husayn ('a) established the practical ideology of Islam and he is the practical model for Islamic movements.

They (that is the Prophet and Imams) wanted Imam Husayn's ideology to be kept alive. They wanted Husayn should reappear every year with those sweet, sublime and heroic summons of his and declare"

Don't you see that what is right and true is not acted upon, and what is wrong and false is not forbidden? [In such conditions] the man of faith should long to meet his true Lord!¹⁵

They wanted the words:

Death is better than a life saddled with indignity,¹⁶ To be kept alive forever, and so also the words:

To me death is nothing but felicity, and life with oppressors is nothing but disgrace,¹⁷ They wanted such other saying of Imam Husayn to be kept alive:

The children of Adam carry the mark of death like necklaces that

---

¹⁵ Bihar al-anwar, vol. 44, p. 381; Tuhaf al-'uqul, p. 176; al-Luhuf, 33; al-Khwarazmi's Maqtal al-Husayn, ii, p. 5.

¹⁶ Ibn Shahr Ashub, al-Manaqib, iv, p. 110; al-Luhuf, p. 50, Bihar al-anwar, vol. 45, p. 50; al-Irbili, Kashf al-ghummah, ii, p. 32.

¹⁷ Bihar al-anwar, vol. 44, p. 381; Tuhaf al-'uqul, p. 176; al-Luhuf, 33.

adorn the neck of damsels![18] Far from us is disgrace and indignity![19]

They wanted to keep alive the memory of such scenes as that of Imam Husayn's confronting a force of thirty thousand men, in a state when he and his family are faced with a great ordeal and declaring in a manly manner -and the world has never seen such a manly personage!

Indeed, that baseborn son of a baseborn father has left me only two alternatives to choose from: the sword or disgrace. And far from us is disgrace! It is disdainful to God, His Messenger and the faithful that we should yield to anything of that kind, and those born of chaste mothers and high-minded fathers and possessing a lofty sense of honor disdain that submission to vile men should be preferred to honorable death![20]

They wanted to keep alive the formative school of Imam Husayn so that the rays of the Husayni spirit may breathe life into this community. Its objective is quite clear.

Do not allow the event of 'Ashura' to be consigned to oblivion! Your life, your humanity, and your dignity depend on this event!

You can keep Islam alive only by its means! That is why they have encouraged us to keep alive the tradition of mourning Imam Husayn, and very rightly! The institution of mourning Husayn ibn 'Ali has a correct philosophy underlying it, a philosophy which is also extremely sublime.

It is fitting that we should do all that we can to endeavor for the sake of this cause, provided we understand its purpose and goal. Unfortunately some people have not understood it.

Without making the people understand the philosophy of Imam

---

[18] Bihar al-anwar, vol. 44, p. 366; al-Luhuf, p. 25.

[19] Al-Luhuf, p. 41; Khwarazmi's Maqtal al-Husayn, ii, p. 7; Ibn 'Asakir, Ta'rikh al-Sham, iv, p. 333; al-Muqarrim's Maqtal al-Husayn, p. 287; al-Harrani, Tuhaf al-'uqul, p. 176; Shaykh 'Abbas al-Qummi, Nafs al-mahmum, p. 149, Mulhaqat Ihqaq al-haqq, xi, pp. 624-625.

[20] Ibid.

Husayn's uprising and without making them understand the station of Imam Husayn, they imagine that if they just came and sat in mourning assemblies and shed tears, without knowledge and understanding, it would atone their sins.

Marhum Hajji Nuri mentions a point in the book, *Lu'lu' wa marjan*. That point is the belief of some people that the reward (*thawab*) for mourning Imam Husayn is so great that it is justifiable to employ any means whatsoever for this end. Nowadays a group which subscribes to the views of Machiavilli in political thought says that ends justify the means. If the end is a good one, it does not matter what means are used to achieve it.

Now these people also say that we have a sacred and exalted goal, which is mourning Imam Husayn and it does not matter what means are used for this end. As the end is a sacred one, it does not matter what the means are: Is it correct to perform *ta'ziyahs* -even *ta'ziyahs* which are vulgar -for this purpose? They ask, 'Do they make the people cry?

If they do, there is so problem with such *ta'ziyahs*.' So also there is no problem if we blow trumpets, beat drums, commit sinful acts, make men dress as women, conjure a wedding for Qasim, or fabricate and forge episodes. Such things do not matter in the tradition of mourning Imam Husayn, which is something exclusive.

Here lying is forgiven, forgery and fabrication are forgivable, making pictures, and dressing men as women is pardonable. Here any kind of sinful conduct is forgivable as the end is most sacred! As a consequence of such thinking, some persons have resorted to such *tahrif* and misrepresentation that are stunning.

About ten or fifteen years ago when I was on a visit to Isfahan, I met a great man, marhum Hajj Shaykh Muhammad Hasan Najafabadi, may God elevate his station. I recounted to him a *rawdah* that I had heard recently somewhere. It was something which I had never heard until that time. Incidentally, this man who had delivered that *rawdah*, an opium addict, had made the people weep profusely with that *rawdah* of his.

In it he recounted the story of an old woman during the reign of Mutawakkil (the 'Abbasid caliph who persecuted the Shi'ah). The woman had set out with the purpose of making a pilgrimage to the tomb of Imam Husayn, which was forbidden at that time and they would cut off the hands of the pilgrims. He went on with the narrative until the point when the old woman is taken and thrown into the river. In that state she cries out for help, calling out, "O Abu al-Fadl al-'Abbas!"

As she is about to drown a horseman appears and tells her to catch hold of his stirrup. The woman takes hold of the stirrups but she says, "Why don't you give me your hand?' The horseman says, "I haven't any hands!" At this point the people wept a lot.

Marhum Hajj Shaykh Muhammad Hasan recounted for me the history of this legend. In a place near the bazaar, in the near abouts of Madrasah Sadr, there used to be held a *majlis* which was one of the major *majalis* of Isfahan and which even the *marhum* Hajj Mulla Isma'il Khwaju'i used to attend. One day there had occurred there an incident.

(It had taken place earlier and he had heard its account from reliable persons.) It involved a well-known *wa'iz*; who himself had recounted it in these words: "One day mine was the last turn to speak from the minbar.

Other speakers had come and each one of them had exerted his skills to make the people weep. Everyone that came would try to surpass his predecessor and having delivered his *rawdah* would descend from the minbar to sit among the audience and watch the art of the succeeding *rawdeh-khwan*. This continued until the time of noon.

I saw that everyone had tried his prowess and together they had drawn out all the tears that the people could shed. What should I do? I thought for a while, and then and there I made up this story.

When my turn came, I went up and related the story, leaving all of them behind. In the afternoon, the same day, while attending another *majlis* in the Char-suq locality, I saw that the one who took to the minbar before me related this same story. Gradually it came to be written in books and appeared in print."

The false and wrong notion that the tradition of mourning Imam Husayn is an exception to all norms, that it is justified to use any means to make the people weep, has been a major factor leading to fabrication of legends and *tahrif*.

Marhum Hajji Nuri, that saintly man and teacher of *marhum* Hajj Shaykh 'Abbas Qummi, who as confessed by Hajj Shaykh 'Abbas himself as well as others was superior to his pupils, was an extraordinarily learned and pious man. In his book he makes the point that if it is a correct notion that the end justifies the means, then one may also justify the following line of reasoning.

One of the Islamic precepts is that bringing delight to the heart of a believer and to do something to make him happy is a greatly commendable act. Such being the case, according to this reasoning, it is justifiable to do backbiting in his presence, as he loves listening to backbiting. And should someone say that it is sinful to do so, the answer will be," No! The purpose is a sacred one and the backbiting is being done to make a believer pleased and happy!"

Marhum Hajji Nuri gives another example. A man embraces a non-mahram woman, which is an unlawful act. We ask him why did you do that? He replies, "I have done it for a believer's delight." The same reasoning can be applied to such unlawful acts as adultery, drinking wine, and sodomy. Isn't this an absurd reasoning?

Wouldn't such a notion destroy the Shari'ah? By God, to think that it is permissible to use any kind of means for making people cry in mourning Imam Husayn is a notion that contradicts everything that Imam Husayn stands for. Imam Husayn was martyred to uplift Islam, as we confess while reciting his *ziyarah*:

I bear witness that you established the prayer, gave *zakat* commanded what is right and forbade what is wrong, and did such *jihad* in the way of God as ought to be done.[21]

Imam Husayn was killed in order to revive Islamic traditions, Islamic laws and regulations, not in order to create an excuse for the violation of Islamic norms. *Na'udhubillah*, we have changed Imam Husayn into a destroyer of Islam: the Imam Husayn that we have conjured in our imagination is a destroyer of Islam.

In his book Hajji Nuri mentions a story that was related to him by one of the students in Najaf, who originally came from Yazd. "One day," he said, "in my youth I made a journey on foot to Khorasan, going by the road that passes through the desert (*kawr*). In one of the villages of Nayshabur I went to a mosque, as I did not have any place to stay.

The imam of the mosque came and led the prayers. Afterwards he went on the *minbar* to make a *rawdah* I was amazed to see the mosque attendant bring a pile of stones which he handed over to the imam. When the *rawdah* started, he ordered the lamps to be put out. When the lamps had been put out, he pelted the stones at the audience and there arose cries from the people. When the lamps were lighted, I saw bleeding heads.

Their eyes were tearful as they walked out of the mosque. I approached the imam and asked him why he had done such a thing. He said, 'I have tested these people. There is no *rawdah* in the world that will make them weep. As weeping for the sake of Imam Husayn has a great reward and *thawab*, I have found that the only way to make them cry is to throw stones on their heads.

This is how I make them weep.' " He believed that the end justifies the means. The end was to mourn Imam Husayn though it should involve

---

[21] Mafatih al-janan, the ziyarah of Imam Husayn ('a) for the nights of 'Id al-Fitr and 'Id al-Adha.

emptying a pile of stones on the people's heads.

Accordingly, this is a particular factor which is specific to this historic event and it has led to much fabrication and *tahrif*.

When one studies history one finds what they have done to this event. By God, Hajji Nuri is right when he says that if we were to weep for Imam Husayn today, we should mourn for him on account of these falsehoods, fabrications and *tahrif*!

There is a well-known book called *Rawdat al-shuhada'*. whose author was Mulla Husayn Kashifi. According to Hajji Nuri, he was the first to write in his book the stories of Za'far the Jinn and the one about Qasim's wedding. I have read this book.

I used to imagine that it contained only one or two of such cases. But afterwards when I read it I saw that the matter was very much different. This book, which is in Persian, was compiled about five-hundred years ago.

Mulla Husayn Kashifi was a scholar and learned man. He has authored several books including the *Anwar suhayli*. His biographical accounts do not indicate whether he was a Shi'i or a Sunni. Basically he was a Chameleon: among the Shi'ah he would pose as an outright Shi'i, while amongst the Sunnis he would pass as a Hanafi.

He was a native of Sabzawar, a Shi'i centre whose people were staunch Shi'is. In Sabzawar he would act as an out and out Shi'i, and at times when he would go to Herat ('Abd al-Rahman Jami was the husband of his sister or sister-in-law) he would give sermons for the Sunnis in the Sunni style. But in Sabzawar he narrated the tragedies of Karbala'.

His death occurred around 910/1504, that is, either at the end of the 9th or the beginning of the 10th century. This was the first book, compiled about five hundred years ago, to be written as an elegiac narrative (*marthiyah*).

Earlier the people used to refer to the primary sources. Shaykh Mufid, may God be pleased with him, wrote the *Irshad* and how sound is his narration! If we were to refer to the *Irshad* of Shaykh Mufid we would not stand in need of any other source.

Tabari, among Sunni authors, has also written about it. Ya'qubi, Ibn 'Asakir and Khwarazmi have also written. I don't know what this unjust man has done! When I read this book I saw that even the names are spurious. He mentions names among Imam Husayn's companions that never existed. He mentions names of the enemy's men which are also spurious. He has turned the factual accounts of the event into fables.

As this was the first book to be written in Persian, the orators in mourning assemblies, who were mostly illiterate and could not use the Arabic texts, would take this book and read from it in the mourning sessions.

That is why the gatherings that are held nowadays to mourn Imam Husayn are called *rawdeh-khwani*. *Rawdeh-khwani* was not in vogue during the time of Imam Sadiq or Imam Hasan 'Askari, nor it was prevalent during the times of Sayyid Murtada [d 436/1044] or even Khwajah Nasir al-Din al-Tusi [d. 672/1273].

Rawdeh-khwani came into vogue since the last five hundred years and it came to be called as such. *Rawdeh-khwani* meant reading from the book *Rawdat al-shuhada'*, a pack of lies. From the time that this book fell into the hands of the people, no one has bothered to study the actual history of Imam Husayn.

Then, about sixty or seventy years ago, there appeared another man, the *marhum* Mulla Darbandi. He took all the contents of the *Rawdat al-shahuda'* and compiled them together with other material, collecting it all in a book called *Asrar al-shahadah*. The contents of this book make one lament for the fate of Islam.

Hajji Nuri writes, "We used to attend the lectures of Hajj Shaykh 'Abd al-Husayn Tehrani (who was a very saintly man) and benefited from his teaching. A sayyid from Hillah, who was a *rawdeh-khwan*, came to meet him and he showed him a book written about the events of

Imam Husayn's martyrdom (*maqtal,* plural: *maqatil*) to see whether its contents were reliable.

This book did not have any beginning or end. Only at one place in it was mentioned the name of a certain mulla of Jabl al-'Amil who was among the pupils of the author of the *Ma'alim al-usul.* Marhum Hajj Shaykh 'Abd al-Husayn took the book to examine it.

First he studied the biographical accounts of that scholar and found that such a book had not been attributed to him. Then he read the book itself and found it to be full of falsehoods. He said to that sayyid, 'This book is a pack of lies.

Don't circulate this book and don't quote anything from it, for it is unlawful to do so. Basically this book has not been written by that scholar and its contents are spurious.' " Hajji Nuri says that the same book fell into the hands of the author of *Asrar al-shahadah* and he copied all its contents into his book, from the beginning to the end!"

Hajji Nuri relates another episode, which is rather touching. Once a man came to author of the *Maqami'*[22] and said to him, "Last night I saw a horrible dream." "What was it?" he asked him. He said, "I saw that I am biting away flesh from the body of Imam Husayn." The scholar trembled on hearing these words.

He lowered his head and thought for a while. Then he said, "Perhaps you are a *marthiyeh-khwan?*". "Yes, I am," he replied. He said, "Hereafter, either abandon *marthiyeh-khwani* altogether or draw your material from reliable books. You are tearing away the flesh Imam Husayn, with these lies of yours. It was God's grace that He showed this to you in a dream."

If one studies the history of 'Ashura' one will find that it is the most vivid and well-documented of histories with plenty of sources. The

---

[22] Marhum Aqa Muhammad Ali was the son of marhum Wahid Behbahani and both of them were great men. Marhum Aqa Muhammad Ali migrated to Kirmanshah where he wielded great influence.

marhum Akhund Khurasani used to say, "Those who are ever after 'new' *rawdahs* should go and read the true accounts, for no one has ever heard them"

One should study the addresses of Imam Husayn ('a) delivered in Makkah -in the Hijaz as a whole -at Karbala', during his journey, as well as the sermons addressed to his companions, the questions and answers that took place between him and others, the letters that were exchanged between him and other people, the letters that were exchanged between the enemies themselves, in addition to the accounts of those (from among the friends as well the enemies) who were present on the occasion of 'Ashura'.

There were three or four persons from among Imam Husayn's companions who survived, including a slave named 'Uqbah ibn Sam'an, who had accompanied the Imam from Makkah and lived to write the accounts pertaining to the Imam's troops.

He was captured on the day of 'Ashura' but was released when he told them that he was a slave.

Humayd ibn Muslim was another chronicler who accompanied the army of 'Umar ibn Sa'd. Of those present on the occasion was Imam Zayn al-'Abidin ('a) himself who has recounted all the events. There is no blind spot in the history of Imam Husayn ('a).

Hajji Nuri refers to a spurious story that relates to Imam Zayn al-'Abidin ('a). According to it when there remained no companion with Hadrat Abu 'Abd Allah ('a), the Hadrat went into the tent of Imam Zayn al-'Abidin ('a) to bid him good-bye. Imam Zayn al-'Abidin ('a) asked him, "Father! How did things come about between you and these people? (that is, Imam Zayn al-'Abidin was unaware of what was happening until that time).

The Imam said to him, "Son, this matter has ultimately led to a battle." 'What happened to Habib ibn Mazahir?, asked Imam Zayn al-'Abidin. "He was killed," replied the Imam. "How about Zuhayr ibn Qayn?"

"He was also killed," replied the Imam. "What happened to Burayr ibn Hudayr?" "He was killed," said Imam Husayn ('a). Imam Zayn al-'Abidin continued naming each of his father's companions one after another and the Imam's reply was the same.

Then he asked concerning the men of Banu Hashim. "What happened to Qasim ibn Hasan?" What happened to my brother 'Ali Akbar?" "What happened to my uncle Abu al-Fadl The answer was the same: "He has been killed." This is a fabrication and a lie. Imam Zayn al-'Abidin, *na'udhubillah*, was not so sick and unconscious as not to know what was going on.

Historians have written that even in that state of illness he rose from his bed and said to Zaynab, "Aunt, bring me my staff and give me a sword." In any case, Imam Zayn al-'Abidin ('a) was one of those who were present on the scene and related the accounts of events.

Truly, we should be penitent for these crimes and treacheries that we are guilty of in respect of Abu 'Abd Allah al-Husayn ('a), his companions, comrades and members of his family, and for effacing all their achievements. He should do penance and then make effort to derive benefit from this most educative source.

Is there any inadequacy in the life of 'Abbas ibn 'Ali as recounted in the reliable *maqatil* (accounts of martyrdom)? The single point that there was no danger to his own life is enough to be a matter of pride for him. Imam Husayn had also told him, "They are only after me, and if they kill me, they will not have anything again anyone else."

At Kufah, when Shimr ibn Dhi al-Jawshan was departing for Karbala', one of those who were present said to Ibn Ziyad that some of his relatives on the mother's side were with Husayn ibn 'Ali. He requested Ibn Ziyad to write a letter granting them amnesty, and Ibn Ziyad wrote it. Shimr belonged to a clan that had remote ties with the tribe of Umm al-Banin (the mother of Abu al-Fadl). Shimr personally brought this letter of amnesty on the night following the ninth day of Muharram.

This wretch approached the camp of Husayn ibn 'Ali and shouted, "Where are my nephews!" (*ayna banu ukhtina?!*).²³ Abu al-Fadl, along with his full brothers, was sitting with Hadrat Abu 'Abd Allah ('a). He remained silent and did not reply, until the Imam said to him, "Answer him, though he be an evil man (*ajibuhu in kana fasiqa*). At the Imam's leave, he answered Shimr, saying, "What do you want?" (*Ma taqul?*). Shimr said, "I have come with some good news for you.

I have brought a letter of amnesty for you from the emir, 'Ubayd Allah. You are now free, and you will be safe if you leave now." Abu al-Fadl said to him, "May God damn you and your emir, as well as the letter that you bring. Do you think we will abandon our Imam and brother for the sake of our own safety?"

On the night of 'Ashura', the first person to declare his loyalty towards Abu 'Abd Allah was his brother Abu al-Fadl. Aside from the foolish exaggerations that are often made, that which is confirmed by history is that Abu al-Fadl was a very wise person, valiant and courageous, tall and most handsome. He had been nicknamed 'The Moon of the *Hashimis*.'²⁴ These things are true. To be sure, he had inherited Ali's courage.

The story is also true regarding his mother, that Ali' had asked 'Aqil, his brother, to propose a woman born of a heroic descent (*waladatha al-fuhulah*)²⁵ who might give birth to son who would be a warrior and man of valour (*li-talidani farisan shuja'ah*).²⁶ 'Aqil had suggested Umm al-Banin. So much of it is true. 'Ali's wish was fulfilled in Abu al-Fadl.

According to one of two reports, on the day of 'Ashura' Abu al-Fadl came to the Imam and said, "Dear brother, now give me the permission.

---

[23] al-Muqarrim's Maqtal al Husayn, p. 252, Bihar al-Anwar, vol. 44, p. 391, al-Luhuf, p. 37

[24] al-Muqarrim's al-Abbas, p. 81; Ibn Shahr Ashub, al-Manaqib, iv, p. 108

[25] al-Muqarrim's al-Abbas, p. 69

[26] Ibsar al-ayn fi ansar al-Husayn alayh al-salam, p. 26

This breast of mine is suffocated and I can bear it no more. I want to sacrifice my life for your sake."

I don't know the reason why Imam responded to Hadrat Abu al-Fadl's request in the manner that he did. Abu 'Abd Allah himself knows better. He said, "Brother, now that you want to leave, try to get some water for these children."

Hadrat Abu al-Fadl had already come to receive the nickname *Saqqa* (water carrier), as earlier, on one or two occasions, at nights he had been able to pass through the enemy's ranks to fetch water for the children in Abu 'Abd Allah's camp. It was not the case that they had not drunk any water for three days and nights.

Access to water had been closed for three days and nights, but during this time they had been able to get some water on one or two occasions, including the night of 'Ashura', when they had taken bath and washed their bodies. Abu al-Fadl consented.

Now note this majestic scene! What greatness! What valour! What a spirit of understanding and self-sacrifice! A lone warrior, alone by himself, advances against a host. The number of men who guarded the river bank was four thousand. He descends along the river bank and leads his horse into the water (all historians have written this).

First, he fills the waterskin that he has brought and lays it on his shoulder. He is thirsty. The air is hot and has been fighting. But as he sits on the back of his horse and the horse stands in water reaching up to its belly, he lowers his hands into water, takes water into them and raises them somewhat towards his sacred lips.

Those who were watching from a distance report that he hesitated for a while. Then they saw that he threw the water back and came out of the river without drinking any. No one knew why Abu Al-Fadl did not drink water there. But when he came out he recited *rajaz* verses which were addressed to himself. Now from these verses they understood why he had not drunk water:

O soul of Abu al-Fadl!
My wish is that you live not after Husayn! Will you have a drink of cold water,
While there stands Husayn, thirsty, near the tents, And about to drink the cup of death!?
Such is not the way of my faith,
Nor that of one who abides in conviction and truth![27]
What would become of manliness? Of honour? Of caring love? And of sharing in the hardship of one's dear ones? Isn't Husayn your Imam, and you his follower?
While Husayn is about to drink the cup of death, Will you have a drink of cold water?
Never! My faith does not permit me to do that! My loyalty does not allow me to do such a thing! Abu al-Fadl changed his route while returning and now he came through the palm groves. Earlier, he had come by the direct way, but he knew that he now carried a precious trust with him.

So he changed his route and all his concern now was to get the water safely to the camp, for it was possible that a single arrow may pierce the waterskin and fail his task of bringing the water to its destination. In the mean while they heard that Abu al-Fadl had changed his *rajaz*. It appeared that something had happened. Now he cried out:
By God!
Even if you sever my right arm,
I will persist in defending my faith,
And the Imam, who is the true one, for certain, the Prophet's grandson, pure and trustworthy![28]
That is, by God even if you cut my right arm I will not flinch from

---

[27] Yanabi al-mawaddah, ii, p. 165; Bihar al-Anwar, vol. 45, p. 41

[28] Bihar al-Anwar, vol. 45, p. 40

defending Husayn. Not much time passed when his *rajaz* changed again:
O my soul, fear not the faithless,
And receive the good news of Almighty's mercy,
In the company of the Prophet, the Master and the Elect, Though, insolently, they should slash my left arm![29]

These *rajaz* verses signaled that his left arm too had been severed. They write that with characteristic dexterity he somehow turned the water-skin and bent himself over it. I will not say what happened thereafter as it is most heart rending.

It is a custom to recount the account of the ordeals of this great human being on the night of *Tasu'ah* (9th Muharram). Let me add that Umm al-Banin, the mother of Hadrat Abu al-Fadl was alive at the time of the event of Karbala', though she was in Madinah at the time. She was given the news that all her four sons were martyred at Karbala'.

This saintly woman would go to the Baqi' cemetery and mourn over her sons. They write that her elegies were so full of pathos that they brought tears to everyone who heard them, even Marwan ibn Hakam, who was the staunchest of the enemies of the Prophet's family.

Sometimes she would remember all her sons and, at times, especially Abu al-Fadl, the eldest of them, who was senior most of the brothers, both in respect of age as well as in respect of spiritual and bodily merits.

I remember one of her two elegies and I will recite them for you. These are the elegiac verses that this grieved mother recited in mourning for her sons (in general, the Arabs recite elegiac verses in a very touching style):
You, who have seen 'Abbas make repeated forays against the base hosts, And following him were the Lion's sons, each a mighty lion!
I have been told, my son's head was struck when his arms were cut, Alas for my Lion's cub! Did a club fall on his head?

---
[29] Ibid.

O 'Abbas! None would have dared to approach it,
Were your sword in your hand!³⁰

That is, 'O observant eye, tell me, you who have been in Karbala' and watched its scenes and observed the moment when Abu al-Fadl, my son of a lion, with my other lion's cubs following him, attacked that cowardly crowd -tell me is it true what I have been told?

They say that when they had cut my son's arms an iron club fell on my dear one's head. Is that true?' Then she says, "Abu al-Fadl! My dear! I know that if you had arms there wasn't a man in the whole world to have the guts to face you! They had the temerity to do that because your arms had been severed from your body.

---

³⁰ Muntaha al-amal, I, p. 386.

Three

Third Sermon 'Ashura – Misrepresentations and Distortions

In the Name of Allah, the Beneficent, the Merciful

All Praise belongs to Allah, the Lord of the worlds and the Maker of all creation, and may Peace and benedictions be upon His servant and messenger, His beloved and elect, our master, our prophet, and our sire, Abu al-Qasim Muhammad, may Allah bless him and his pure, immaculate, and infallible Progeny.

I seek the refuge of Allah from the accursed Satan:

> *"So for their breaking their compact We cursed them and made their hearts hard; they would pervert the words from their meanings, and they forgot a portion of what they were reminded of." (5:13)*

We stated earlier that the history of an event of such greatness as Karbala' has been subject to distortion at our hands both in respect of its external details as well as its meaning. By distortion of outward form we mean the accretions that we have piled up on the corpus of its history which have obscured its bright and luminous visage and disfigured its beautiful countenance. We cited some instances in this regard.

Distortions of Meaning

Regrettably this historic event has also been distorted in respect of its meaning, and corruption of meaning is much more dangerous than corruption of external detail. That which has made this great event ineffectual for us is the corruption of meaning, not that of external detail. That is, the evil effect of distortions in meaning is greater than those pertaining to external details.

What is meant by distortion of meaning? Without adding a single word or deleting a single word, it is possible to misinterpret a statement in such a manner that it gives a meaning exactly contrary to its real meaning.

I will give just one small example to illustrate this point. At the time that the early Muslims were building the Mosque of Madinah, 'Ammar Yasir was working hard, making an extraordinary amount of sincere effort. Among the reports that are of a definite authenticity is the one that the Noble Messenger (S) said to him at the time:

'Ammar, you will be killed by the rebellious faction.[31]

The term 'rebellious faction' (*al-fi'at al-baghiyah*) is Qur'anic, and it occurs in a verse which states that if two faction of Muslims fight one another and one of them is rebellious, one must take a stand against the rebellious faction and join on the side of the other faction so that the matters are set right.

'If two factions of believers fight, make peace between them,

---

[31] al Halabi, Sirah v2, p77

> **but if one of them rebels against the other, fight the one which is rebellious until it returns to God's command."** *(49:9)*

The statement, made by the Noble Messenger concerning 'Ammar, gave him great prestige. Accordingly, during the Battle of Siffin, when 'Ammar fought on the side of Imam 'Ali ('a), Ammar's presence in 'Ali's troops was considered a strong point in 'Ali's favour.

There were people with a weak faith who, until 'Ammar had not been killed, were not convinced that it was right for them to fight on Ali's side and lawful to kill Mu'awiyah and his soldiers.

But on the day that 'Ammar was killed at the hands of Mu'awiyah's soldiers, suddenly a cry rose from all sides that the Prophet's prophesy had come true.

The best evidence of the unrighteousness of Mu'awiyah and his companions was that they were the killers of 'Ammar and the Prophet had informed years ago through his statement that 'Ammar will be killed by a rebellious faction.[32]

On this day it became quite clear that the Mu'awiyah's troops represented the rebellious faction, that is, one which was unjust and unrighteous, and that justice lay on the side of 'Ali's army. Hence in accordance with the express injunction of the Qur'an one had to join the battle on 'Ali's side and against Mu'awiyah's army.

This incident demoralized Mu'awiyah's troops. Mu'awiyah, who always tried to make a headway by resorting to cunning and subterfuge, resorted to a misinterpretation. It was not possible to deny that the Prophet had made such a statement concerning 'Ammar, because perhaps there were at least five hundred persons who could bear witness that they had heard this statement from the Prophet himself or from someone who had heard it from the Prophet.

---

[32] Musnad, Ahmad b. Hanbal, v2, p199

Accordingly, it was not possible to deny the fact of the prophesy concerning 'Ammar. The Syrians protested to Mu'awiyah, for it were they who had killed 'Ammar and the Prophet had said that he would be killed by a rebellious faction. Mu'awiyah told them, "You are mistaken. It is true that the Prophet said 'Ammar will be killed by a rebellious faction and army.

But it were not we who killed 'Ammar." They said, "He was killed by our warriors." "No," he said, "'Ammar was killed by 'Ali who brought him here and provided the causes of his death."

'Amr ibn 'As had two sons. One of them was a worldly person like himself. The other one was a youth who was relatively a man of faith and he did not agree with his father's ways. His name was 'Abd Allah. 'Abd Allah was present in a gathering where this sophistry was put into effect. 'Abd Allah said, "What a false argument that it was 'Ali who has killed 'Ammar, as he was among his troops.

If that is so, then it was the Prophet who killed Hamzah, the Doyen of the Martyrs, as Hamzah was killed due to his presence in the Prophet's troops." This enraged Mu'awiyah and he said to 'Amr ibn As, "Why don't you check this ill-mannered son of yours!" This is what is called distortion of meaning.

How is the Meaning of Events and Facts Distorted?

Historical events and facts have on the one hand certain causes behind them, and, on the other, they are inspired by certain goals and motives. Misrepresentation of a historical event lies in ascribing to it causes and motives other than what they have actually been, or in attributing to it goals and motives other than what they in fact were.

For instance, you visit someone who has recently returned from a pilgrimage to Makkah. The purpose you have in mind is that it is mustahab to visit a hajji and so you go to see him. Someone makes a remark about your motives for the visit, describing them as an intention to propose your son's marriage with his daughter under the pretext of visiting a hajji returning from Makkah.

This is how he misrepresents your motive and purpose. This is what misrepresentation means.

The historic event of Karbala' had certain causes and motives behind it, as well as certain sublime goals. We Muslims and followers of Husayn ibn 'Ali have misrepresented this event in the same way as Mu'awiyah ibn Abi Sufyan distorted the meaning of the Prophet's statement concerning 'Ammar.

That is, Imam Husayn ('a) had certain goals and motives for staging his uprising and we have ascribed to him some other motives and goals.

The Character of A Sacred Movement

Abu 'Abd Allah ('a) made an uprising that was of unusual greatness and sanctity. The uprising of Abu 'Abd Allah possessed all the characteristics that make an uprising sacred, so much so that it is without a parallel in the entire history of the world. What are those characteristics?

The first condition of a sacred movement is that it should not have a purpose and end that is personal and pertaining to the individual but one which is universal, covering the entire humanity and human species.

At times persons make uprisings for personal goals, and sometimes they may launch a movement for the sake of society, or for the sake of mankind, for the sake truth, or for the sake of justice, equality and monotheism, and not for some personal goal. In such cases the struggle and movement is no longer for a personal cause.

One who wages such a struggle represents all human beings. That is why men whose actions and movements were not for the sake of personal motives and for the sake of humanity or for the sake of truth, justice and equality, and for the sake of tawhid and knowledge of God and for the sake of faith, are honored and loved by all people.

And that is why the Prophet (S) said: "Husayn is from me and I am from Husayn"[33] We also say, "Husayn is from us and we from Husayn." Why? Because Imam Husayn, may Peace be upon him, took a stand 1328 years ago[34] for our sake and for the sake of all mankind. His uprising was sacred and holy and it transcended personal goals.

The second condition for an uprising to be sacred is that it should be inspired by a powerful vision and insight. To explain, suppose there is a society who people are unaware, ignorant, and without understanding.

There appears among them a man of vision and understanding who understands their ailments and their remedies a hundred time better than they do. At a time when others fail to understand and see, the man of vision sees very early and distinctly what other people fail to see at all. He comes forward and takes a stand.

Years pass. Twenty, thirty or fifty years later the people wake up and find out why he had risen up and they understand the sacred goals that he had sought to attain whose value and worth was not visible to their fathers and ancestors twenty, forty or fifty years ago.

To give an example, the marhum Sayyid Jamal al-Din Asadabadi [Afghani] launched an Islamic movement about sixty or seventy years ago in the Muslim countries (his death occurred in 1310 H./1892-93, fourteen years before the Constitution Movement in Iran). When you read today the history of this man, you see that he was truly a lone and solitary figure.

He knew the maladies of Muslims and their remedy while the people

---

[33] al Mufid, al Irshad, p249, Alam al Wara, p216, Ibn Shahr Ashub, al Manaqib, v4, p71, Hilyat al abrar, v1, p560, Kashf al Ghummah, v2 pp10,61, Mulhaqt Ihqaq al haqq, v11, pp 256-279

[34] This sermon was delivered in the year 1389 H, corresponding to Farvardin 1348 (March-April 1969)

themselves did not. He was insulted and ridiculed by the people and they did not support him. Now after sixty or seventy years when the facts of history have become clearer we see that he understood things at that time which the people of Iran, ninety-nine out of a hundred, did not.

Read at least two of the letters written by this great man. One of them was written to the marhum Ayatullah Mirza Shirazi Buzurg, may God elevate his station. The other was an open letter to the 'ulama' of Iran and is like a manifesto. Or read the letters written by him to marhum Hajj Shaykh Muhammad Taqi Bujnardi at Mashhad, or to a certain eminent scholar of Isfahan or Shiraz.

See how well he understood the problems and how clearly he saw things, how well he knew the character of colonialism and what effective measures he took for awakening this ummah (pay no attention to things that are still said about him by some agents of colonialism, for as the proverb goes, 'this henna has lost its color'!).

His movement was sacred because it was launched by a man who appeared during a difficult era and who saw the reality behind the appearances which was invisible to and hardly understood by his contemporaries.

The movement of Imam Husayn is such a movement. Today we understand fully the character of Yazid and the implications of his rule. We know what Mu'awiyah did and what were the schemes of the Umayyads. But the Muslims of that era, ninety-nine out of a hundred, did not understand these things, especially due to the absence of the media of the mass communication media which exist nowadays.

The people of Madinah did not understand the situation that existed. They came to know the character of Yazid and the implications of his caliphate when Husayn ibn 'Ali was killed. They were shocked and they asked themselves why he had been killed. They sent a delegation to Syria consisting of some eminent persons of Madinah and led by a man named 'Abd Allah ibn Hanzalah, known as "Ghasil al-Mala'ikah."

Making the journey from Madinah to Syria when they reached Yazid's court, after staying there for some time they came to know the realities of the situation. On returning to Madinah they were asked as to what they had seen. They said, "All that we can tell you is that so long as we were in Damascus we were afraid lest stones should rain on our heads from the heaven."

They told them they had seen a caliph who drank wine openly, gambled, and played with hounds and monkeys and had incestuous relations with women of his family.

Abd Allah ibn Hanzalah had eight sons. He said to his townsmen, "Whether you rise up or not, I will make an uprising even if I have to do it alone with my sons." He fulfilled his words. In the uprising of Harrah against Yazid he sent forth his sons to fight.

They were martyred and he himself was martyred after them. 'Abd Allah ibn Hanzalah was not aware of the conditions two or three years earlier when Imam Husayn departed from Madinah. Where was he at the time when Husyan, as he prepared to leave Madinah, was saying:

One should bid farewell to Islam when the *ummah* is afflicted with such a ruler as Yazid?

Husayn ibn 'Ali had to be killed and the Muslim world had to receive a shock so that the likes of 'Abd Allah ibn Hanzalah, the Ghasil al-Mala'ikah, and hundreds of people like him in Madinah, Kufah, and other places may open their eyes and say that Husayn ('a) was right in saying what he said.

The third characteristic of a sacred movement is its solitary and exclusive character; that is, it is like a flash of lightening in total darkness, a cry in the wilderness of silence, and a movement in the sea of absolute stillness. In conditions of total repression when the people cannot speak out, when there is total darkness, despair, absence of hope, and absolute silence and stillness, there appears suddenly a man and he breaks the magic silence and stillness.

He makes a movement and it is like a flash of light in the midst of surrounding darkness. It is then that others begin to stir and gradually start moving behind him and following him. Wasn't the uprising of Husayn such a movement? Yes, it was. Such was the movement that Imam Husayn launched. But what were his objectives in launching it?

Why were the Infallible Imams so insistent that the tradition of mourning Husayn ibn 'Ali ('a) should always remain alive? There is no need for us to look far for the reasons. Husayn ibn 'Ali himself has declared the reasons behind his movement:

Indeed, I have not risen up to do mischief, neither as an adventurer, nor to cause corruption and tyranny. I have risen up solely to seek the reform of the Ummah of my grandfather (s).

He says in most explicit terms: "Our society has become corrupt and the ummah of my Grandfather has become degenerate. I have risen up to carry out reform and I am a reformer."

I want to command what is good and stop what is wrong, and (in this) I follow the conduct of my grandfather and my father, 'Ali ibn Abi Talib.

Don't you see that righteousness is not acted upon and vice goes unforbidden. In such a situation, the man of faith yearns for the meeting with his Lord ... I see death as nothing but felicity and life under oppressors as nothing but disgrace.

Imam Husayn ('a) says, "I have risen up to carry out *amr bil ma'ruf*, to revive the faith, and to struggle against corruption. My movement is one which is Islamic and aimed at reform."

But what we say is something else. We have made two skillful manipulations which are very amazing (I don't know whether I should say skillful or ignorant). In one of these cases, we said that Husayn ibn 'Ali rose in order to be killed for the sake of the atonement of the sins of the ummah.

Now if someone were to ask us as to the source of this notion, whether it was Imam Husayn ('a) himself who said such a thing or if it was the Prophet or some Imam, we cannot cite any authority. But still we keep on insisting that Imam Husayn got killed so that our sins are atoned. I don't know whether we have borrowed this notion from Christianity. Muslims have unwittingly adopted many ideas from Christendom which are contrary to Islam.

One of the doctrines of Christianity is the notion of the crucifixion of Christ as a sacrifice made for the sake of the atonement of man's sins. Jesus is called 'the Sacrifice,' and it is an essential part of the Christian doctrine that Jesus went upon the cross for atoning the sins of his people. They have made Jesus carry the burden of their sins!

However, we did not suspect that this notion belongs to Christianity and that it is consistent neither with the spirit of Islam nor with the statements of Husayn ('a) himself. By God, it is a calumny if we ascribe such a thing to Aba 'Abd Allah ('a)! By God, should one attribute such a notion to Husayn ibn 'Ali while he is keeping a fast in the month of Ramadan and claim that Husayn's martyrdom was for the sake of such a purpose and should he ascribe such a statement to him, his fast would be void for ascribing a falsehood to the Imam. Abu 'Abd Allah rose to struggle against sin, whereas we said that he rose in order to be a refuge for sinners!

We claim that Imam Husayn founded an insurance company to guarantee security to sinners! He has insured us against the consequences of sin in return for our tears. All that we have to do is to shed tears for him and in return he guarantees immunity to the sinners.

Now one could be whatever one liked to be, one could be an Ibn Ziyad or 'Umar ibn Sa'd, as if one 'Umar ibn Sa'd, one Sinan ibn Anas, and one Khuli were not enough! Imam Husayn wanted that the likes of Khuli and 'Umar ibn Sa'd should proliferate in the world and so he came and announced: 'O people, be as evil as you can be, for I am your security!'

There is a second misrepresentation involved in interpreting the event of Karbala'. According to it, Imam Husayn made an uprising and was killed in order to carry out a special command that was solely addressed to him. He was told to go and get martyred. So his action does not relate to us and it is not something which can be followed and emulated: it does not relate to those precepts of Islam which are general and universal.

See, what a great difference there is between what the Imam declares and what we say! Imam Husayn cried out that the causes and motives of his uprising are matters that coincide with the general principles of Islam. There was no need for a special order. After all special orders are given in situations where the general prescription is not adequate.

Imam Husayn declared in unequivocal terms that Islam is a religion that does not permit any believer (he did not say, an Imam) to remain indifferent in the face of oppression, injustice, perversity and sin. Imam Husayn established a practical ideology which is the same as the ideology of Islam. Islam had set forth its principles and Husayn put them into effect.

We have divested this event of its ideological character. When it is shorn of its ideological character, it is no more capable of being followed, and when it can not be followed, one cannot make any use of Imam Husayn's teaching and draw any lesson from the event of Karbala'. We have rendered this event barren from the viewpoint of being beneficial and useful.

Could there be a worse kind of treachery? This is the reason why I say that the distortion in the meaning of the event of 'Ashura' is a hundred times more dangerous than textual corruption.

Why did the Infallible Imams (and there are even traditions from the Noble Messenger in this regard) want this movement to be kept alive? that it should not be consigned to oblivion?-that the people should mourn Imam Husayn? What was the objective that led them to issue this command?

We have distorted that objective, declaring that their only goal was that the mourning ceremonies are to be held for the sake of offering consolation to Hadrat Zahra', may Peace be upon her. Although she is with her great son in Paradise, we imagine that she is continually restless and full of sorrow, so she should be given consolation by the mourning of such worthless people as us! Can there be a greater insult of Hadrat Zahra' than this notion?

Some others say that Imam Husayn was murdered without any guilt at Karbala' at the hands of a group of aggressors and this was a tragedy. It is true that Imam Husayn was killed without any guilt. But is this all there is to the event that an innocent person was murdered by a group of aggressors!? Every day a thousand innocent persons are killed and wiped out throughout the world by criminals, and this is of course a tragic fact.

But does this kind of death have such a value that one should go on expressing sorrow over it and continue to mourn it year after year, for years, or rather for centuries, for ten and twenty centuries, expressing sorrow and regretting that Husayn ibn 'Ali was killed without guilt and that his innocent blood was shed for no reason by aggressors? But who can dare say that Husayn ibn 'Ali's death was in vain and his blood was shed futilely?

If one can find anyone in the whole world who did not allow one drop of his blood to be wasted, that is Husayn ibn 'Ali. If you can find anyone in the whole world who did not let one particle of his personality to go waste it is Husayn ibn 'Ali. He set such a high value for every single drop of his blood that it is indescribable!

If you take into account the amount of wealth that has been and is spent for his sake and will continue to be spent until the day of Judgment, you will see that humanity has spent billions and trillions for every drop of his blood.

Can anyone say that a man wasted his life whose death, for ever and ever, sends out tremors through the castles of the oppressors?-that his blood went in vain? Is his martyrdom to be saddening for us because Husayn ibn 'Ali was killed in vain?

It is we, wretched and ignorant people that we are, I and you, whose lives go waste. We should grieve for ourselves! You insult Husayn ibn Ali when you say that his life was lost in vain! Husayn ibn 'Ali is someone about whom it is said.

Indeed you have a station with God which cannot be attained except through martyrdom. Did Husayn ibn 'Ali desire to die a vain death when he aspired for martyrdom?

The Imams have exhorted us to keep alive the tradition of mourning over Husayn ibn Ali because his goal was a sacred goal. Husayn ibn 'Ali established a school, and they wanted his school to remain alive and flourish.

You will not find a practical school of thought in the whole world that may be likened to that of Husayn ibn 'Ali ('a). If you can find a single another example of Husayn ibn 'Ali, you may ask why we should revive his memory every year.

If you can find another example of that which was manifested in Husayn ibn 'Ali during the event of 'Ashura', in those ordeals and taxing conditions, of the meaning of tawhid, of faith, of the knowledge of God, of perfection, convinced faith in the other world, of resignation and submission, of fortitude and manliness, of self contentment, of steadiness and steadfastness, of honor and dignity, of the love and quest for freedom, of concern for mankind, of the passion to serve humanity- if you can find a single example in the whole world, then you may question the need to refresh his memory every year. But he is unique and without a parallel.

Keeping alive the memory of his name and his movement is for the purpose that our spirits may be illumined by the light of the spirit of Husayn ibn 'Ali ('a).

If a tear that we shed for him should signify a harmony between our souls and his spirit, it represent a brief flight that our spirit makes along with Husayn's spirit. Should it create within us a little glow of his valor, a particle of his free nature, a particle of his faith, a particle of his piety, and a small spark of his tawhid, such a tear has an infinite value.

They have said that it has the worth an entire world even if it is so small as the 'wing of a gnat.' Believe it! But that is nor a tear shed for a pointless death, but a tear for the greatness of Husayn and his great spirit, a tear that signifies harmony with Husayn ibn 'Ali and of movement in his steps. Yes, such a tear has an incalculable worth even if it is so small as a gnat's wing.

They wanted this practical ideology to remain for ever before the people's view, to witness that the Prophet's family are a proof and testimony of the truthfulness of the Prophet himself. If it is said that a certain Muslim warrior displayed great faith and valor in such and such a battle against Iran or Byzantine, for instance, it is not so much of an evidence of the Prophet's truthfulness as when it is said that the Prophet's son did such and such an act.

A leader's family is always subject to more suspicion and doubt than any of his followers. But when we observe the family of the Prophet at the highest summit of faith and sincerity, that is the best evidence of the Prophet's truthfulness. No one was so close to the Prophet (S) like 'Ali ('a). He grew up by the Prophet's side. No one had a faith in the Prophet like him or was more dedicated to the Prophet. This is the first evidence of the Prophet's truthfulness.

Husayn is the Prophet's son. When he manifests his faith in the Prophet's teaching it is a manifestation of the Prophet himself. Things which are always declared by human beings verbally but are rarely observed in practice are clearly visible in Husayn's being. What makes a human being so undefeatable? Subhan Allah! See the heights to which a human being can rise!

See how undefeatable is the spirit of the human being whose body bears wounds from head to foot, his young sons have been cut to pieces before his very eyes, he is suffering from extreme thirst and when he looks up at the sky it appears dark in his eyes, he sees that the members of his family will be taken captive, he has lost all that he had and all that has remained for him is his own undefeatable spirit.

Show me such a spectacle of human greatness in an event other than Karbala' and I will celebrate its memory instead of Karbala! Accordingly, we should keep alive the memory of such an event, of a group of seventy-two persons who defeated the spirit of a host of thirty thousand. How did they inflict such a defeat? Firstly, though a minority facing certain death, not a single one of them pined the enemy's side.

Yet some men from the thirty thousand pined their ranks, including one of their commanders, Hurr ibn Yazid Riyahi and another thirty. This indicates the moral victory of this group and the defeat of the other one. 'Umar ibn Sa'd took certain measures in Karbala' which disclose his moral defeat. In Karbala' 'Umar ibn Sa'd's men refrained from a man-to-man encounter during the battle. At first they complied in accordance with the custom prevalent in those days, before launching an all-out attack and shooting arrows.

The man-to-man fight was a kind of contest in which one man from one side fought a man from the other. After several men were killed in these encounters with the companions of Imam Husayn, strengthening their morale, 'Umar ibn Sa'd ordered his men to refrain from man-to-man fights.

When did Abu 'Abd Allah come to the field for the final battle? Imagine, it is afternoon on the day of 'Ashura'. Until this time there were still several of his companions who offered the prayers with him. He has been very busy from the morning until the afternoon of that day as it was he, most of the time, who has brought the bodies of his companions from the battlefield and placed them in the tent of the martyrs.

He himself has rushed to the side of his companions in their last moments and it is he himself who consoles and reassures his family members. Apart from all this, there is his personal grief for the dear ones that he has lost. He is the last of all to come into the field of battle. They imagine that it would be a simple task to deal with Husayn in such a circumstance.

But he does not give a moment's reprieve to any contestant that dares to come forward to combat him. 'Umar ibn Sa'd then cries out: "Woe to you! Do you know whom you are fighting? This is the son of the most fatal of Arab warriors. He is the son of 'Ali ibn Abi Talib. By God, his father's soul is in his body.

Don't fight him singly!"

Wasn't this an indication of defeat? Thirty thousand men combat against a single man, lonely and solitary, who has suffered all those sorrows and ordeals., and who has been through the arduous and grueling labors of the day, thirsty and hungry, and he defeats them and makes them flee.

They faced a defeat not only against the sword of Abu 'Abd Allah but also his logic and eloquence. Abu 'Abd Allah delivered two or three sermons on the day of 'Ashura' before the commencement of his battle. These sermons are truly amazing.

Those who practice the act of oration know that it is not possible for someone in an ordinary state to say things which are sublime or at the height of sublimity. One's spirit must be in a state of fervor, especially if the oration is of an elegiac character. It is only with a heart burning with feeling that one can deliver a good elegy.

If one wants to compose a ghazal, he must be strongly moved with the passion of love so as to say a good ghazal. If one wishes to compose epic poetry, he must be moved with warlike emotions.

When Abu 'Abd Allah began his address, especially the sermon that he made on the day of 'Ashura', which is one of the most elaborate of his sermons, 'Umar ibn Sa'd was alarmed by the effect it might have on his men's morale. The Imam alighted from his horse and mounted a camel in order to make the sermon, as he wanted to make his voice heard better from a higher point.[35]

Words, which are truly reminiscent of the sermons of 'Ali ('a). Aside from the sermons of 'Ali we won't find a more powerful and vibrant sermon in the whole world. He spoke three times. 'Umar ibn Sa'd was frightened lest Husayn's sermon should change the minds of his troops.

The second time when Abu 'Abd Allah started to address them, due to the defeatist morale of the enemy, Umar ibn Sad ordered his men to hoot and beat their mouth with their hands so that no one could hear Husayn. Is that not an evidence of their defeat and the sign of Husyan's victory?

If a man has faith in God, in *tawhid*, if he has a link with God and faith in the other world, single-handedly he can inflict a moral defeat on a host of twenty and thirty thousand. Is this not a lesson for us? Where can you find another example of it?

Who else can you find in the whole world who could utter two sentences of that sermon in conditions in which Husayn ibn 'All spoke, or for that matter two sentences like the sermon of Zaynab ('a) at the city gates of Kufah?

If our Imams have told us to revive this mourning every year and to keep it alive for ever it is for the purpose that we may understand these points, that we may realize the greatness of Husayn, so that if we shed tears for him it is out of understanding.

Our knowledge of Husayn elevates us. It makes us human beings, free men, followers of truth and justice, and real Muslims. The school of Husayn is a man-making school, not a school that produces sinners.

---

[35] al Masudi, Muruj al Dhahab, v3, p69

Husayn is the bastion of righteous conduct, not a citadel for sin and sinfulness.

The historians report that at daybreak on the day of 'Ashura', after offering the prayer with his companions, he turned to them and said, "Companions, get prepared. Death is nothing but a bridge that takes you across this world into another, from a world that is very coarse, hard and base to one that is sublime, noble and gentle."

These were his words. But now observe his conduct. The reports do not come from Husayn ibn 'Ali but from those who have chronicled the events. The episode has been reported even by Hilal ibn Nafi', who was accompanying 'Umar ibn Sa'd as his chronicler.

He says, al Husayn ibn 'Ali was astonishing to me. As the time of his martyrdom drew nearer and his ordeals became severer, his countenance appeared to be more refreshed and ruddier, like someone about to meet his beloved."

Even in the last moments when that accursed wretch approached him to sever his sacred head, he says, "When I approached Husayn ibn 'Ali and my eyes fell on him, the light and burnish of his face so gripped me that I forgot my intention to kill him:

The light of his face and its awe-inspiring beauty so gripped me that I was distracted from the thought of killing him.

They write that Abu Abd Allah had chosen a point for his combat which was nearer the tents of the womenfolk. That was for two reasons. Firstly, he knew the unmanly and inhuman character of the enemies. They lacked even the sense of honor to spare the tents of their attacks as it was he whom they were fighting.

Therefore he wanted to restrain them from attacking his camp so long as he was alive and had the strength to stop them. He would make a frontal attack and they would flee. But he would not pursue them but return to guard the tents of his womenfolk from any assault.

Secondly, so long as he was alive he wanted the members of his family to know that he was alive. Accordingly, he had chosen a point from where his voice could be heard by them. Whenever he returned after making an attack he would stand at that point and cry out:

There is no power or strength save that which derives from God, the Exalted and the Almighty.

His cries would reassure the women who knew that the Imam was still alive. The Imam had told them not to come out of the tents as long as he was alive (Don't believe those who say that the women kept running out every now and then. Never.

The Imam had ordered them to remain in the tents as long as he was alive). He had told them that they must not make any untoward utterance which might reduce their reward with God. He had told them that they would find deliverance and that their ultimate end would be a good one, that God will punish their enemies.

They did not have the Imam's permission to come out of their tents, and they did not. Husayn ibn Ali's sense of manly honor and their own sense of feminine honor did not permit them to come out.

Accordingly, when they heard the Imam utter *'La hawl wala quwatta illa billahil aliyyil azim'*, they felt reassured. And as the Imam had come back to them once or twice after bidding them farewell, they still expected the Imam to return.

In those days they used to train Arabic horses for the battlefield, as the horse is an animal that can be trained. Such a horse would show a particular reaction when its master were killed. The members of Abu 'Abd Allah's household were in the tents awaiting the Imam, that he might return to them once again and they might see his angelic visage one again. Suddenly they heard the sound of the neighing of the Imam's horse.

They rushed to the tent's door imagining that the Imam had come. But they saw the horse without its rider with its saddle overturned. It was then that the children and the women raised the cries of *Wa*

Husaynah! and *Wa Muhammada!* They surrounded the horse and each of them began to mourn for him.

Mourning is part of human nature.

When a person wants to express his grief he mournfully addresses the heaven, or an animal, or some person. The Imam had told them that they must not weep or lament so long as he was alive. But of course they could mourn him when he died. And so in that state they began their lamentations.

They write that Husayn ibn 'Ali had a daughter named Sukaynah, whom he loved greatly. Later she grew up to become a learned lady of letters much revered and respected by all scholars and literary men.

This child was very dear to Abu 'Abd Allah ('a) and she too had an unusual love for her father. They write that this child uttered some sentences in the way of mourning which are very heartrending. In a mournful tone she addressed the horse and said:

O my father's stallion, my father was thirsty when he went out. Did they give him water or was he killed thirsty?'

That was at the time when Abu 'Abd Allah lay fallen on the ground.

Four

Fourth Sermon: Ashura – Popular Distortions and our Responsibility

In the Name of Allah, the All-Beneficent, the Most Merciful.

All Praise belongs to Allah, the Lord of the worlds and the Maker of all creation, and may Peace and benedictions be upon His servant and messenger, His beloved and elect, our master, our prophet, and our sire, Abu al-Qasim Muhammad, may Allah bless him and his pure, immaculate, and infallible Progeny.

I seek refuge with Allah from the accursed Satan:

> *"So for their breaking their compact We cursed them and made their hearst hard; they would pervert the words from their meanings, and they forgot a portion of what they were reminded of." (5:13)*

Our discussion concerning the distortions *(tahrifat)* in popular accounts of the historical event of Ashura consists of four parts:

First, the meaning of distortion *(tahrif)* in general.

A description of the distortions that have taken place in regard to the historic event of 'Ashura and their examples.

The factors responsible for these distortions and the causes that lead to *tahrif* in general and the special factors that have been particularly at play in relation to this historic event.

Our responsibility' in regard to these distortions, that is, the 'duty of the *'ulama'* as well as that of the common people.

Of these four, we have already discussed the first three parts in the previous sessions, and tonight, with God's grace, we will discuss the fourth topic.

To be certain, during the course of time gradually there have taken place distortions in this very great historic event, and there is no doubt that here we have a responsibility: to combat these distortions.

To state it more clearly, and to put it in somewhat self-important terms, it may be said that our generation has a mission to fight against these distortions and in misrepresentations of 'Ashura. But before we may discuss the responsibility of the scholars of the ummah (in other words, the *khawass*) and the responsibility of the people (that is, the *'awamm*), I would like to mention two points in the way of introduction.

The first point is that we should examine the past to see who has been responsible for these distortions, whether it were the scholars who were responsible for it or the common people. Next, what is our responsibility to today and who is to shoulder it?

Who has been responsible for it in the past? Usually in such cases the *'ulama* blame the people and the people put the blame on the *'ulama*. The *'ulama* say that the guilt lies with the people and their ignorance. They are so ignorant, ill-informed and un-worthy that they only deserve to be fed with such nonsense. They do not deserve to know the truth and the facts.

I heard it from the *marhum* Ayatullah Sadr, may God elevate his station, that Taj Nayshaburi would say absurd things from the *minbar*. Someone objected to him, saying, "What are these things that you say? You receive such big audiences, why don't you say some sensible things?" He replied that the people did not deserve it. Then he produced, so to speak, a 'proof' to substantiate his assertion.

The common people, the masses, also have an argument against the *'ulama* and the clerics which they often use. They say, "When a fish begins to rot, the rotting begins at the head. The scholars are like the head of the fish and we its tail." However, the fact is that in this case the responsibility and the guilt lies both upon the *'ulama* as well as the laity.

One should know that the common people too share a responsibility in such cases. In cases such as this, it is the people who let the truth to be obliterated and spread superstitious nonsense.

There is a well-known tradition which is considered reliable by scholars. A man asked Imam Sadiq (a) concerning the Qur'anic verse:

"And among them are the illiterate folks who know not the Book but only vain hopes and nothing but conjectures." (2:78)

Here God is critical of the common people from among the Jews. Although He refers to them as having been uneducated, unlettered and illiterate, nevertheless He considers them blameworthy. The questioner, while admitting that the *'ulama'* of the Jews' were indeed responsible, asks the Imam as to why the common people among them were held guilty. Was it not a valid excuse that they were illiterate commoners? The tradition is an elaborate one.

The Imam replies that such is not the case. He answers that there are certain matters that do require learning and which can only be understood by the learned and which illiterate people do not comprehend. Concerning such issues one may say that the common people are not responsible as they have not acquired learning in religious subjects. True, at times they may be held responsible for not having acquired education, and this could be an argument against them.

However, if there are cases where they have no responsibility, that is in issues which require the study of books and proper instruction under teachers. One who has never had any teacher and has never gone to school is not held responsible in such matters.

However, there are issues which a normal human being can understand with his natural faculty of a sound mind. Here it is not necessary for one to have gone to the school, to have read books and have had teachers. In other words, it does [not] require one to have a diploma or a degree or even to have received middle-school education. All that is needed is sanity and a sound mind.

Thereafter, the Imam gives an example. Suppose there is an *'alim* who preaches the people to be pious and Godfearing while he himself acts in a manner contrary to piety and Godfearing. He preaches what he himself does not practice and the people observe this contradiction between his word and deed. The Imam points out that it is not necessary for one to be educated and learned in order to see that such men are not worthy of being followed.

The common people among the Jews would observe these things with their own eyes and understand them with their minds *(wadtarru bi ma'arifi qulubihim)*.[36] With their natural intelligence they could perceive that one must not follow such persons, but in spite of that they would follow them. Therefore they were responsible and guilty.

There are some matters that do not require any education or training or any linguistic expertise in any particular language such as Arabic or Persian or any training in any of such subjects as grammar, law, jurisprudence, logic or philosophy.

All that is needed is the natural gift of intelligence and they (the common people among the Jews) did possess this. They perceived

---

[36] Al-Tabrisi, al-Ihtijaj, vol.2, p.457.

these things with their natural intelligence. The Noble Prophet (s) has a saying which is one of the profoundest because of its innate self-evident character. He said:

The value of works depends solely on intentions, and everyone's recompense depends on his intentions.[37]

It means that the significance and worth of one's actions depends on one's intentions. If you do something unintentionally you are not guilty if it is something bad and if it is something good you do not deserve any reward.

Now if someone were to come and relate a dream and a story about someone who is forgiven his sins and admitted to the highest stations of paradise due to something that happened to him in a condition of unconsciousness in which his will and intention had played no role whatsoever, or rather his real intentions were quite the opposite, should we accept such a thing?

Does it require book learning? Does it need literacy or the knowledge of Arabic? Only repentance and a return to God can free one from his sins:

"Verily good deeds obliterate evil deeds." (11:114)

It is good deeds that wipe out the traces left by evil deeds. But involuntary actions are not such. However, 'we fail to use our God-given intelligence to make correct judgements.

In some books they have written that once upon a time there was a robber who used to waylay travellers, rob them and kill them. One day he came to know that a caravan of pilgrims bound for the holy shrine in Karbala was on its way. He came and hid himself in a mountain pass lying there in wait to waylay the pilgrims bound for the shrine of Imam

---

[37] Al-Majlisi, Bihar al-anwar, vol. 7, p. 225; al-Jami' al-saghir, vol. 1, p. 3.

Husayn, to rob them of their belongings and to kill them if necessary.

While he waited for the caravan to reach, suddenly he fell asleep. The caravan came and passed by while he remained asleep. In that state he saw a dream. It was the scene of the day of resurrection and he was being taken towards hell. Why? Because he had not performed a single good deed in his life. All he had done was wickedness and crime.

He was taken to the verge of hell but hell refused to accept him. Why? Because as this man slept by the wayside as the pilgrim caravan passed, the dust raised by the feet of the pilgrims of Imam Husayn's shrine had settled on his body and clothes.

As a result of this involuntary act all his sins were forgiven without his having any conscious intention, or rather despite his intention to kill the pilgrims, and contrary to the declaration of the Prophet that "the value of actions depends solely on intentions, and everyone's recompense depends on his intentions." [There is even a couplet that has been composed on the theme.]

Indeed, hell shall not touch a body, whereupon lies the dust of the feet of Husayn's pilgrims!

It is a nice line poetically, but is unfortunately untrue from the viewpoint of the teaching of Imam Husayn.

The second point, which I must mention before describing this responsibility and duty relates to the dangers that lie in these distortions. Let us briefly discuss the dangers that lie in distortion of facts. We have already discussed the various kinds of distortion that have occurred in relation to the historic event of 'Ashura and the factors responsible for such distortions. It is possible that some people might think, 'After all what is wrong with *tahrif*?'

What harm can it do and how can it create any danger?' The answer is that the danger of *tahrif* is extraordinarily great. *Tahrif* is an indirect blow which is more effective than a direct one. If a book is corrupted (whether in respect of its wording, or its meaning and content) and it is a book of guidance, it is transformed into a book that is misleading. If it is a book of human felicity it is transformed into a book of human wretchedness. If it is a book that edifies and elevates human beings, as a result of corruption it is changed into one that brings man's fall and degeneration. Basically it alters the very form of reality and not only makes it ineffective it has a reverse effect.

Everything is prone to certain hazards which are related to its nature. The Noble Prophet (s) said:

There are three hazards for religion: the scholar of evil conduct, the tyrannical leader (ruler), and the person who is diligent in practicing religion but is ignorant.[38]

That is, there are three dangers for religion: 1) scholars who are evil and vicious in their conduct; 2) leaders who are tyrannical and unjust; 3) devout persons who are ignorant. The Prophet has considered them hazards for the faith.

In the same way that plants and animals are affected by certain pests and diseases, and in the same way as the human body is prone to certain diseases and disorders, religion, creed and faith are also prone to certain dangers.

Distortions of the faith, which are brought about by two out of the three categories of people mentioned by the Noble Prophet, that is, scholars of evil conduct and ignorant and sanctimonious persons, are a hazard for the faith and are destructive for religion. Corruption and distortion alter the content of a message of deliverance and the people who accept it as the truth derive an opposite result.

Ali (a), a figure with all that greatness, has a strangely distorted personality in the outlook of some people. Some people know Ali (a) only as an athlete. At times some people of very suspect motives publish pictures of Ali that show him bearing in hand a two-tongued

---

[38] Al-Jami' al-saghir, vol. 1, p. 4.

sword, like a pythons tongue, and with facial features and expression one does not know from where they have got them. It is definite that a picture or statue of Ali or that of the Prophet never existed.

They have painted such a strange face that one can hardly believe that it is the same Ali famous for his justice, the Ali who wept at nights for the fear of God. The face of a devout man, of someone who is used to nightly worship, of someone who engages in *istighfar* at nights, the face of a sage, a judge, a man of letters is a different face.

There is another thing which is quite popular especially amongst us Iranians. We refer to the Fourth Imam (a) as "Imam Zayn al-'Abidin-e *Bimar*" (i.e. the sick one). In no language do we ever come across the epithet *bimar* along with the name of Imam Zayn al-'Abidin. Such an epithet does not exist in Arabic.

He has a number of appellations, one of which is *al-Sajjad* (i.e. one who prostrates a lot), another is *Dhu al-Thafanat* (i.e. one who has callouses on his forehead, due to prostrations). Do you find any book in Arabic that may contain an epithet synonymous with the word *bimar* for the Imam?

Imam Zayn al-'Abidin (a) was only ill during the days of the episode of 'Ashura (perhaps it was an act of providence meant to save the Imam's life and to preserve the progeny of Imam Husayn) and this very illness saved his life.

Several times they wanted to kill the Imam, but as he was seriously ill, they would leave him saying, *Innahu li-ma bih*[39] i.e., Why should we kill him. He is himself dying. Who in the world has not fallen ill at some time or another during his life?

Apart from this instance of his illness, see if you can find any other reference stating that Imam Zayn al-'Abidin was sick. But we have

---

[39] Bihar al-anwar, vol. 45, p. 61; A'lam al-wara, p. 246; ash-Shaykh al-Mufid, al-Irshad, p. 242.

pictured Imam Zayn al-'Abidin as someone chronically ill, pale faced, suffering from fever and as someone bent with weakness and always carrying a walking stick and someone who moans as he walks !

The same distortion and lie about the Imam's figure has led some people to continually groan and moan and make themselves appear as chronically sick so that people may revere them for that and say, "Look at him, he is just like Imam Zayn al-'Abidin the *Bimar!*" This is distortion. Imam Zayn al-'Abidin was not any different from Imam Husayn (a) or Imam Baqir (a) in respect of physical health and constitution.

The Imam lived for forty years after the event of Karbala' and he was quite healthy like others and was not different from Imam Sadiq (a), for instance, in this regard. Why should we then call him "Imam Zayn al-'Abidin the *Bimar*"[40]

Imamate means being a inodel and an exemplar. The philosophy of the Imam's existence is that he is a human being of a superhuman calibre, like the prophets, who introduced themselves in these words so

---

[40] In the late Ayati (r), may God have mercy upon him, we have lost an invaluable asset. Five or six years ago this great man gave a lecture on the method of tabligh in one of the monthly sessions of a religious association. It was published in the second volume of Guftar-e mah. There he raised this very issue. He said, "What is this absurd notion that we attribute sickness to Imam Zayn al-Abidin? We have given such an appellation to the Imam that anyone who hears it imagines that the Imam was sick all his life." Then he related an episode that had occurred recently He said, "Some time ago I read an article in one of the periodicals where the author had complained about the plight of the government and government employees, stating that most of the government servants and officials were either incompetent or corrupt. They were either competent and corrupt, or honest and incompetent." He had cited verbatim the words of the author; who had written, "Most of the government officials are either of the type of Shimr or that of Imam Zayn al-'Abidin-e Bimar; whereas we need persons who are competent like Hadrat Abbas." He meant that Shimr was corrupt and competent, whereas Imam Zayn al-'Abidin-e Bimar was pious but -na'udhubillah -incompetent, and that Hadrat Abbas was both pious and competent. See how an apparently small distortion leads to such a great deviation.

that the people may follow them as higher models of humanity:

> *"I am only a mortal like you, (and) it has been revealed to me that your God is One God." (18:110)*

However, when the countenance of these figures is distorted to a great degree they are no more capable of serving as models. That is, instead of being beneficial, following and emulating such imaginary figures gives an opposite result. Thus we have seen briefly the great danger that lies in *tahrif*. Actually *tahrif* is an indirect blow and a stab in the back.

The Jews are the world champion of *tahrif*. No people in world history have carried out *tahrif* to the extent that they have done. For the same reason no one has ever delivered a great blow to humanity by distorting facts and fabricating falsehoods.

Our Responsibility and Mission:

You should know that we have a serious responsibility in this regard, especially in the present times. One cannot serve the people with a distorted version of the truth, neither was it possible in the past. It was unproductive also in the past, but its harm was lesser.

Its harm is much greater in this era. Our greatest responsibility is to see what distortions have occurred in our history; to see what distortions have occurred in the presentation of our eminent figures and personalities, and what misinterpretations have occurred in the Qur'an.

There has been no textual corruption in the Qur'an. It means that not a single word has been added to it nor a word has been deleted from it. However, the danger of distortion of the meanings of the Qur'an is as serious as any textual corruption.

What is meant by distortion of meanings of the Qur'an? It means interpreting the Qur'an in a wrong and misleading manner. Such a thing should not be permitted to take place. We should see what kind of distortions have taken place in our history in historical episodes such as the historic event of 'Ashura, which must always remain a source of lesson and education for us, being a document of moral and social training and education. We should combat such distortions.

The Duty of the 'Ulama and the People:

What is the duty of the *'ulama'* of the Ummah in this regard and the duty of the common people, the masses?

I want to make a general remark concerning the responsibility of the *ulama'*. The deviation of an *'alim* lies in always confronting passively the weak points and shortcomings of the people. Spiritual, moral and social weak points are a kind of sickness. In bodily illness the sick person is usually conscious of his illness and he himself seeks his own treatment.

But in spiritual illnesses that which makes things difficult is that the sick person does not know that he is sick. On the contrary he considers his illness a sign of health. He even has a liking for his illness. It is not the case that individuals are conscious of their weak points and accept them as such; rather they consider them as their strong points! It is the *'alim* who understands the weak points of his community

When an *'alim* is faced with a weak point of the community he has two alternatives before him:

1. He may struggle against these weak points, and such a person is called a reformer *(muslih)*. A reformer is one who fights against the weak points of the people. The people usually do not like him.
2. He may consider it a difficult and formidable task to combat the weak points of the people. He may conclude that there is not only

no reward to be obtained in fighting the people's weak points, but there are also disadvantages. Accordingly, he exploits their weakness.

It is here that he becomes an instance of 'the vicious scholar' (*faqih fajir*) who according to the Noble Prophet (s) is one of the three hazards and pestilences of the faith.

I will not discuss other problems here but will confine myself to the issue of the event of 'Ashura. The common people have two weak points in relation to the mourning ceremonies held for Imam Husayn (a).

One of them is that -to the extent I have come across in my own experience (and I have not yet encountered any exception) -usually those who arrange and organize the mourning gatherings (*majalis*), whether they are held in mosques or at homes, want the *majalis* to draw good attendance. They are satisfied if there is a substantial crowd and are unhappy if the attendance is sparse. This is a weak point.

These sessions are not held to draw crowds. Our purpose is not to hold a parade or a march past. The purpose is to become acquainted with the truths and to fight against distortions. This is a weak point which the speaker has to reckon with.

Should he fight this weak point or should he exploit it like Taj Nayshaburi? Should he wish to combat this weak point it would not be compatible with the objectives of the organizers and holders of the *majlis* as well as with the wishes of the audience who like to get together and love tumult and fanfare.

Should he want to exploit this weak point then all that may bother him is how to draw larger crowds. It is here that an *'alim* stands at a crossroad: now that these people are fools and have such a weak point, should I exploit it, or should I struggle against it and go after the truth?

Another weak point present in the mourning gatherings -which is mostly from the people's side and has fortunately become lesser -is that profuse and loud weeping is regarded as the criterion of their success. After all the speaker on the *minbar* must relate the sorrowful accounts of the tragic events.

While these accounts are related, the people are expected not merely to shed tears: the mere shedding of tears is not acceptable; the *majlis* must be rocked with cries of mourning.

I do not say that the *majlis* should not be rocked with mourning; what I say is that this must not be the objective. If tears are shed as a result of listening to facts and the *majlis* is rocked with mourning by descriptions of real history without false and fabricated narratives, without distortion, without conjuring companions for Imam Husayn that did not exist in history and who are unknown to Imam Husayn himself (as they were nonexistent), without attributing such children to Imam Husayn as did not exist, without carving out enemies for Imam Husayn that basically had not existed -that is very good indeed.

But when reality and truth are absent, should we go on making war against Imam Husayn by fabricating falsehoods and lies?

This is a weak point of the common people. What is to be done? Should it be exploited? Should we exploit it for our interests and take them for a ride? Should we, like Taj Nayshaburi, say that as the people are stupid, we should make use of their stupidity? No! Our greatest responsibility and the *'ulama's* biggest duty is to struggle against the weak points of society. That is why that the Noble Prophet (s) said: -

When heresies and fabrications appear in my Ummah, the *'alim* must declare what he knows, otherwise he will be cursed by God.[41]

That is: when falsehoods and fabrications appear and when things become popular which are not part of the religion, things which the Prophet (s) has not prescribed, it is the duty of the learned to declare the truth even if the people do not like it. And may curse of God be

---

[41] Safinat al-bihar, vol. 1, p. 63; Usul al-Kafi, vol. 1, p. 54.

upon him who hides the facts. The Noble Qur'an itself has declared in stronger terms:

> *"Those who conceal what We have revealed of the clear signs and guidance, after We have made them clear for the people in the Book, God shall curse them and they will be cursed by all the cursers." (2:159)*

It means, the learned who conceal the truths declared by Us, who know the facts but conceal them and refrain from expressing them, may the curse of God be upon them and the curse of everyone who curses. The duty of the *'ulama* during the era of the last prophesy is to struggle against *tahrif*. Fortunately the means for such a task are also available and there are, and have been, persons among the *'ulama* who combat such weak points.

The book *Lu'lu' wa marjan* was written on this very topic of the event of 'Ashura and I have mentioned it earlier. It is by the *marhum* Hajji Nuri (may God be pleased with him) and its purpose is precisely to carry out a campaign in this regard, a most sacred duty which has been fulfilled by that great man, whose work is an instance of the first part of the above-mentioned *hadith*:

When heresies and fabrications appear in my Ummah, the *'alim* must declare what he knows ...

It is the duty of the *'ulama* to state in clear terms the facts relating to this case to the people even if they do not like it. It is the duty of the *'ulama* to combat falsehoods. It is the duty of the *'ulama* to expose the liars. The jurists (*fuqaha*) have made certain remarks concerning the issue of back-biting (*ghibah*). They say that there are certain exceptions where back-biting is permissible. Among cases relating to these exceptions is one where all the major *'ulama* have committed this kind of *ghibah*, considering it necessary and even obligatory.

This is the case of *jarh,* where the standing of a narrator *(rawi)* is critically examined. Suppose a person narrates a tradition from the Prophet (s) or from one of the Imams (a). Is one to accept his statements immediately? No. One must investigate his background to see what kind of man he was, whether a truthful person or a liar.

If you discover a weak point in the life of this person, a shortcoming, a defect, an instance of lying or misconduct, it is not only lawful for you but even obligatory *(wajib)* to discredit this person in your books.

This is called *jarh.* Although it is *ghibah* and it amounts to casting disrepute on someone -which is in general not a lawful thing to do whether the subject is dead or alive -but in this case where the matter is that of distortion of the truth and its *tahrif,* one must discredit him and the liar must be exposed and discredited.

Someone may be a great scholar in a certain field, such as Mulla Husayn Kashifi, who was a very learned religious scholar. But his *Rawdat al-shuhada* is replete with lies. No one has been spared of his lies. Even Ibn Ziyad aud 'Umar ibn Sa'd are victims of his lies.

He has written that Ibn Ziyad gave fifty camel-loads *(kharwar)* of gold to 'Umar ibn Sa'd so as to make him go to Karbala' to do what he did. (Anyone who hears such a story might think that if such is the case one cannot put much blame on 'Umar ibn Sa'd. There are many who would do such. a thing if given fifty camel-loads of gold.)

There is a general agreement about Mulla Darbandi that he was a good man. Even *marhum* Hajji Nuri, who criticizes his book, and with justification, says that he was a good man. This man was sincerely devoted to Imam Husayn (a) and it is said that whenever he heard Imam Husayn's name mentioned tears would come into eyes.

He was also quite well-versed in *fiqh* and *usul al-fiqh.* He imagined himself to be a jurist *(faqih)* of the first rank. However; that was not the case. He was a jurist of second or at least third rank. He wrote a book named *Khaza'in* (lit. 'treasures') which is a complete course in *fiqh* and has been published. He was a contemporary of the author of the *Jawahir* (lit. 'jewels'). He asked the author of the *Jawahir* as to what title he had given to his book. He said, *'Jawahir.'*

As the title of his own book was *Khaza'in,* he said, "There are many of such *jawahir* in our *khaza'in.*" However, the *Jawahir* has been reprinted ten times and there is no jurist who does not use it or can do without it. The *Khaza'in* was printed only once and thereafter no one went after it. Although it has a thousand pages, it is not worth more than the paper used to print it.

This man, in spite of being a scholar, wrote the *Asrar al-shahadah* in which he has totally distorted the event of Karbala, altering it and twisting it out of shape, making it ineffective and inconsequent. His book is full of lies. Now should we keep our silence about him because he was a scholar, a pious man and devoted to Imam Husayn? Should not Hajji Nuri give his opinion about his *Asrar al-shahadah?* Of course, he must be subjected to *jarh* and this is the duty of an *'alim.*

We beseech God, the Blessed and the Exalted, to lead our hearts towards the truth, to forgive us the sins which we have committed through *tahrif* and otherwise, to grant us the ability to carry out successfully the duty and mission that we have in this field.

www.ingramcontent.com/pod-product-compliance
Lightning Source LLC
Chambersburg PA
CBHW021450070526
44577CB00002B/341